ALSO BY ROSS ELLENHORN

Parasuicidality and Paradox

How We Change

PURPLE CRAYONS

PURPLE CRAYONS

The Art of Drawing a Life

Ross Ellenhorn

HARPER WAVE

An Imprint of HarperCollinsPublishers

HarperCollins books may be purchased for educational, business, or sales promotional use. For information, please email the Special Markets Department at SPsales@harpercollins.com.

FIRST EDITION

Designed by Nancy Singer

Library of Congress Cataloging-in-Publication Data has been applied for.

ISBN 978-0-06-314380-7

22 23 24 25 26   LSC   10 9 8 7 6 5 4 3 2 1

To Andrew

"Innovators always seek to revitalize, extend and reconstruct the status quo in their given fields, wherever it is needed. Quite often they are the rejects, outcasts, sub-citizens, etc. of the very societies to which they bring so much sustenance. Often they are people who endure great personal tragedy in their lives. Whatever the case, whether accepted or rejected, rich or poor, they are forever guided by that great and eternal constant—the creative urge.**"**

—John Coltrane

66Human beings were given a secret and that secret was not how to begin, but how to begin again.**99**

—Elie Wiesel

CONTENTS

HAROLD
and the
PURPLE
CRAYON

by

Crockett

Johnson

HAROLD'S BIRTH YEAR

Crockett Johnson's children's book *Harold and the Purple Crayon* first appeared in bookstores in 1955. There's no date more appropriate for its publication. At the peak of a decade, on the spine of the century, where more years would soon fall behind than lay ahead, and where no one could imagine the quantum speed of our adventure from one millennium to the next, it teeters like . . . well . . . a book on the tip of an index finger. Telling a story about living one's life as art and the powers that block us from doing so, about serious play and suffocating seriousness, and about what it means to feel alive inside and what deadens our existence, it's also about 1955 in America, and all that lay before and—presciently—all that lay ahead, as each of us struggles to draw meaningful and resilient existences on the blank pages of our yet unlived lives.

If you haven't had the good fortune to read it, *Harold and the Purple Crayon* tells the story of a boy who is always alone with his crayon. When he doesn't use it to draw, the pages are nothing but bare whiteness. When he deploys it, he draws a world around him through which he embarks on a hero's journey that eventually leads him home. Harold draws what he needs and what he yearns for, and along the way he inadvertently draws disasters, then draws solutions to those disasters.

There's no doubt that little Harold is influential (my favorite example of his influence is that Prince, the genius musician and songwriter, fell in love with purple when his mother read him Johnson's book). But he's more a minor celebrity than a blockbuster star like Winnie (the Pooh) and the Cat (in the Hat). That might be one reason why *Harold and the Purple Crayon* can be mistaken for a really great book that does a fantastic job of urging children to use their imaginations, but not more than that.

Harold and the Purple Crayon does offer more, however—much more. From the first squiggle on that ever-recognizable dark crimson cover to the last empty page, this book digs deep.

Like all heroes, Harold has many ups and downs on his journey, and many challenges that he faces head on. In fact, the plot of his story is formed by a series of crises: Harold plummeting scarily from an image he's drawn, rising from those descents by drawing a way to get back up, or just pushing forward by drawing a future. So, at its outer crust, *Harold and the Purple Crayon* is about personal fortitude, those attributes we typically call grit and resilience. But it's also about something more layered than just bouncing back or bootstrapping it.

We can recover and move forward from challenges and crises by complying with the demands of others, conforming to what everyone else is doing, and thoughtlessly following the leader. Or we can get up in a way that is self-possessed and assures that the person we were before the difficult event is still who we are after the worst of it is over. Johnson's book is about this latter form of fortitude, a refined style of connation we call dignity.

But it's also deeper than that.

At the mantle of this book is a lesson about how an innovative approach to challenges is an important avenue to building a dignified life. Harold's beautiful purple renderings are not art for art's sake; he draws them to sustain who he is.

Yet Harold is more than a psychological MacGyver, combining found materials in original ways to stay afloat. He's being original because, for him, originality is what it's all about. Harold holds as sacred the unique intuitions, impulses, values, and tastes that render him Harold. Thus the thing he uses to protect his dignity and the thing he's protecting that makes him dignified are the same: his one-of-a-kind soul.

Harold and the Purple Crayon is a celebration of what I call "sacred originality." This idea—that each of our unique inner lives is worth nurturing and protecting—is really the core message in Johnson's book.

Well, almost . . .

Harold and the Purple Crayon is also about how *hard* it is to maintain our sacredness as original beings: the perseverance and the courage it takes to do so, often in the face of powerful forces that want us to do just the opposite. Harold repeatedly falls out of artful living into struggles with an inanimate and hollow existence, one in which he either sacrifices his originality to conform or experiences moments of isolation and dislocation. His story is thus as much about what it takes to feel alive in our humanity as it is about the terror of what happens when we don't, and how we recover from periods of emptiness in ways that resist the call to just follow along.

This makes *Harold and the Purple Crayon* a very modern book, and one with particularly American undertones. It reflects a shifting in the American character, described by David Riesman and his colleagues in their book *The Lonely Crowd*, written just five years before Harold's birthday. Considered one of the great works of American sociology, *The Lonely Crowd* is a sort of early riff on a theme that would repeat itself throughout the 1950s, one that reverberates through Johnson's book. Riesman et al. were concerned with where we place the psychological GPS that directs the course of our lives. For them, Americans had moved from following a "tradition-directed" map, charted by elders, to "inner-directedness," in which they hold the purple crayon of their destiny in their hands, to an emerging mode that is "outer-directed," piloting their decisions by homing in on what their neighbors were doing. For Riesman and his colleagues, Americans were losing "their social freedom and their individual autonomy in seeking to become like each other." I think the author of *Harold and the Purple Crayon* was worried about the same thing.

Crockett Johnson began his career as an illustrator in the late 1930s creating cover art for *New Masses*, a leftist magazine focused primarily on fighting the growing menace of fascism, a political force that quashes inner-directedness in service of conformity. Johnson later moved to more established magazines, and then to his famous *Barnaby* cartoon series. *Harold and the Purple Crayon* was a sort of return to the subject of Johnson's earlier work. Stripped of overt political statements, the book remains a salutation to the liberating and even disobedient elements in creativity as well as a warning about the serious danger of a world that was becoming more uniform and standardized, one in which its citizens were losing touch with their originality, relinquishing their purple crayons to others.

People in 1955 were engaged in "a kind of blind, desperate clinging to safety and security at any price," as Richard Yates describes it in *Revolutionary Road*, a novel about suburban life that takes place that year. *Harold and the Purple Crayon* is partly about that price and largely about a way to renege on paying it.

The force of uniformity, not just as a psychological stance but as a way of life, was marching fast and powerfully in 1955. The first McDonald's in the McDonald's empire opened that year, the original link in a chain that would cover this country (and, eventually, the world) and supply a uniform set of flavors comfortingly the same at every location. Coca-Cola was first produced in cans, in order to more easily distribute millions of identical syrupy concoctions.

It was also the year Disneyland opened its gates, a terrain of manufactured imagination, an automated, assembly-line approach to our most inner-directed experiences. The Disney enterprise had grander ambitions than just a park in Anaheim. That same year, *The Mickey Mouse Club* first graced the screens of television sets throughout the country, promoting a whitewashed and white-skinned version of a homogenized adolescence to millions. The 1950s have been dubbed the "age of advertising" and the "decade of consumerism," and TV played no small part in that. In 1950, approximately six million homes had TVs; five years later, the number was closer to forty-six million, offering advertisers unprecedented access to consumers. This was the age of the "culture industry," as Theodor Adorno called it, in which artistic acts, those human practices that we typically associate with individual originality, were becoming standardized.

Adorno was a member of the Frankfurt School, a group of mostly Jewish intellectuals, many of whom escaped Germany for the United States. Their thinking was very influential in Harold's time. And their concerns about the growing orientation toward uniformity came from a freshly horrific example.

In 1955, the Holocaust survivor and Nobel laureate Elie Wiesel finished his memoir *Night*, a recounting of his experiences in the concentration camps at Auschwitz and Buchenwald to later become an invaluable historical marker of the atrocities there.

Let's not forget that *Harold and the Purple Crayon* was written only ten years after the closing of those camps—the ghastly banality of "just following orders" ringing an alarm in people's ears. People then were not only worried that we were becoming sheeplike in our behavior, everyone robotically following the same standard of how to act and what to own, but that the consequence of losing touch with the thing that makes us most human was the thingification—the *de*humanization—of others. Feeling hollow inside, we were seeing others as similarly hollow. This is what uniformity breeds: an emptying of our most sacred inner selves and a blindness to the sacred originality in others. As people were becoming more alienated (a well-worn term in the 1950s), they were as "out of touch with [themselves] as [they were] out of touch with any other person," wrote the Frankfurt School alumnus Erich Fromm in 1955 in *The Sane Society*, "experienced as things are experienced."

Here enters Martin Luther King Jr., catapulted into fame in Harold's birth year by his involvement in the Montgomery bus boycott, the largest civil rights protest in American history so far. A scholar of American religion, King's idea that there was something sacrosanct about the "content" of each of our unique "characters" was central to his thought, calling this holy site "the sacredness of human personality." For him segregation was profanely antihuman precisely because it "ends up relegating persons to the status of things." "Any law that uplifts human personality is just. Any law that degrades human personality is unjust," King wrote in his "Letter from a

Birmingham Jail." "All segregation statutes are unjust because segregation distorts the soul and damages the personality."

On December 5, 1955, King spoke to a crowd of five thousand at a Montgomery church, just four days following the arrest of Rosa Parks for refusing to relinquish her seat on bus 2857. In that speech, like many others to come, King relied less on the Bible to make his case than on newer testaments, born from the Enlightenment. "We are here in a general sense because first and foremost we are American citizens," he said, "and we are determined to apply our citizenship to the fullness of its meaning." That theme would remain throughout his work, tying the notion of something sacred about our personalities to defaulted "promissory notes" of our founding documents, as he put it in the famous "I Have a Dream" speech: broken guarantees of the opportunity to be self-determined.

And King was right. The Declaration of Independence and the Constitution are indeed guarantees (unmet, regularly revoked, yet proven to expand and expanding), and what they guarantee is a life of invigorated opportunity. Our founding documents proclaim as "self-evident" that each of us is our own sovereign—a human-size territory, with its own boundaries, its own culture—with the right to make manifest our own potential greatness. We are a land of inventors and innovators, and our DNA is thick with the code of immigrants, people who took the risk to leave the familiar for the unknown, who believed this land would offer a chance for them to build lives of their own design. While often corrupted by a prioritizing of financial success, and a dangerously rugged and crass individualism, the sanctification of originality is deeply embedded in the American dream, one in which "self-made" means to make a *self*, to create, to actuate the original world inside oneself for all the world to see.

By turning to the founding documents as sanctifiers of such sacred originality, King was doing something very American. In fact, his acts of civil disobedience were influenced by one of America's great philosophers on our cherished original innerness, the transcendentalist Henry David Thoreau.

About fifteen miles from where King would study for his doctorate, and just fifty years following the signing of the Declaration of Independence—at the very spot where the first shots of the American Revolution were fired, no less—transcendentalism thrived in the towns and farms around Concord, Massachusetts. Ralph Waldo Emerson was its most famous father, and Thoreau, its most celebrated offspring. In its religious manifestation, transcendentalism saw God in nature, and our own ability to be fully ourselves as the most natural behavior and so the most godly. For them, it is only our tendency toward conformity and our overreliance on institutions and authority that leads us astray, leaving us "Gods in ruins," as Emerson put it; living "lives of quiet desperation," in Thoreau's famous words. Conformity, for them, was a kind of sin. Originality was holy.

The transcendentalists promoted an inner-directed character

because it matched the times: a self-reliant person who could fully take advantage of the promise of a life in pursuit of liberty and happiness (there's little sunlight between Riesman and the transcendentalists on this point). Their work was a kind of collaboration with the Founding Fathers: *You do the job of writing a constitution that makes the individual sovereign, and we'll finish the job by forming an individual who has the right traits to handle this sovereignty.* Reaching that goal required individuals to maintain their ability to "live sturdily," in Thoreau's words, in order to improvise their own course through life. And they were looking for a kind of individualism that wasn't purely characterized by brute ruggedness but had more refined traits, like imagination, intuition, curiosity, spontaneity, and heart.

But the transcendentalists didn't create the idea that there is something sacred in each person's originality. Neither did King, nor our founding documents. To understand sacred originality in American life is to understand it as a sort of ubiquitous aquifer filled from disparate sources, flowing underfoot before springing up from seemingly nowhere, fortifying the flowers and loosening the hard earth just enough for other springs to surge. We invented the hoedown, rock and roll, break dancing, and pussy hats, and we've born such originators as Woody Guthrie, Eleanor Roosevelt, and James Brown, not because of a singularly identifiable basin of thought or art but because our progress as a democracy has always depended on the repeated sanctification of originality, its advocates often unsung patriots—many seen as downright un-patriotic, in fact.

A little over a decade after Emerson's death in 1882, and many miles from the pristine waters of Massachusetts, the sound of sacred originality would powerfully fill the thick humid air around the parks along the Mississippi River in New Orleans.

Arguably the most American of American music, jazz is based on the ideal of constant, in-the-moment innovation. It's a music that defies uniformity, no longer jazz when it conforms. To get there, it relies on the human properties the transcendentalists most cherished: not the unalterable score we each follow in a regimented manner but spontaneity, intuition, and fresh-swinging awe.

In large part invented by the children and grandchildren of slaves living together under continued subjugation, this self-reliantly impro-visational music was also a kind of survival manual: a message about how to stay a person in the face of profound dehumanization. That (and of course many other obvious things) makes the progenitors of jazz different from the philosophers in Concord, one of whom lived "deliberately" in something like a sharecropper's shack, but built by *choice*, on that famous pond less than a mile from his wealthy friends and his mother's warm and welcoming home. Coming from places of trauma and oppression, jazz is a kind of Holy Ark of creativity, aimed to protect the sacred in every personality from the most hor-rific elements in the forces of uniformity. Yet this, too, was about living "sturdily," not only for the purpose of a deeper life but for the soul-defending goal of safeguarding what is most revered within us.

Farther, farther we go, to the Pacific Ocean and San Francisco, six decades since Buddy Bolden first played jazz with his bands on the banks of the Mississippi, where sacred originality is still raging in a new form, as a group of mostly white poets and writers, many recent transplants from New York City, were cultivating a new form of poetry and literature, one that was greatly influenced by bebop and the great transcendentalist-influenced poet Walt Whitman. Their style was called "beat," as in beat poetry, then beatnik, and then the beat generation.

The beat poets were worried about the threat of mass culture, consumerism, corporate conglomerates, and the war industry on the "Spontaneous Me," as Whitman, decades earlier, had titled one of his poems. The beats rightly saw in jazz an art form that resisted the forces of uniformity, and they sought to emulate it in their writing. Indeed, Allen Ginsberg's renowned poem *Howl* reads like a jazz version of a transcendental standard, but more despondent, more pessimistic that the "quiet desperation" of conformity was now ubiquitous, as the Moloch of capitalism sacrificed its young. Ginsberg read *Howl* for the first time at Six Gallery in the Filmore District. It was 1955.

When Harold was born, people complained so much about conformity that we can mistake 1955 for a drought year for sacred originality and end up forgetting something very important: That, like Ginsberg's poem, these complaints howled. In some circles, the very American counterpunch to the march of uniformity was wildly creative, with profound implications for the years ahead. The film *Rebel Without a Cause*, a story about teenage anomie in the age of uniformity and suburban sprawl, was a hit. People were going to see *Inherit the Wind*, a play about the stagnant, dangerous pull of what we now call "science deniers" and their attack on our liberties for the sake of the uniformity of a singular religious explanation for everything. Disability and women's rights activist Helen Keller won the Academy Award for her biographical documentary (the play, *The Miracle Worker*—also based on her biography—was published in 1956 and produced on Broadway in 1959). Chuck Berry's "Maybellene," considered one of the first rock-'n'-roll songs, was number five on the 1955 *Billboard* overall top ten chart. The first lesbian rights group, the Daughters of Bilitis, formed. The comedy album *At Sunset*, a recording of Mort Sahl, who made it his business to criticize conformity (once quipping that Brooks Brothers stores don't need mirrors, since customers can just stand in front of each other), was recorded in 1955 and is in the Library of Congress, distinguished as the earliest recorded example of stand-up comedy. Miles Davis formed the First Great Quintet, with a young John Coltrane on saxophone. James Baldwin was putting the finishing touches on his first novel, *Giovanni's Room*, which explores sex between men and bisexuality, and would be critically acclaimed when published the next year. Abstract expressionism, with its emphasis on an abandonment of conventional form, was in its heyday. Pop art was just beginning, its subjects often mimicking and mocking the reproductive process of mass culture. Martha Graham produced her dance piece *Seraphic Dialogue*, telling the story of Joan of Arc's initial moments of inspiration, with sets designed by the ever-inventive Isamu Noguchi. For the more conventional, you had John F. Kennedy's *Profiles in Courage*, which located the loftiest of human attributes in scenarios in which an individual, acting alone, prevailed over conformity's arrow quiver of ridicule and ostracism. Though diminished by its genre, *Harold and the Purple Crayon* is in fact very much part of the literature, art, activism, and thinking of this time, a proponent of sacred originality but also a warning about a giant wave of outer-directedness cresting over humanity.

You don't know what you treasure until that thing is threatened. As Johnson and his cohorts scrambled to protect their valuables, they spoke loudly about the right to act originally as a thing to be cherished and guarded with our lives, messages for future generations bottled in literature, art, music, philosophy, theology, the social sciences, and protest movements. Johnson joined with many others to celebrate originality before it was too late, his book one such message, placed in his own bottle, then sent out to sea.

The year 1955 is only a life-span ago, but ideas that connect our originality to our humanity are still getting lost, rerouted by materialism, disassembled by the digital revolution, distorted by mass advertising and mass consumerism, estranged by the prioritizing of identity over humanity in the teachings in our universities, and many other trends. This really worries me, since I don't know what to stand for, if not the original self in all of us.

And that's why I think a deep dig into Harold's world is very important. Read in a certain light, there's a realistically inspirational message from Johnson in there. It urges us to see that a creative approach to life is indelibly sewn into the American fabric, and it encourages us to love and fight for this gloriously original and resilient fiber even though it's stitched to many threads that are less giving, many of them barbed.

I want to pass the message in *Harold and the Purple Crayon* on to you, with of course my own thoughts and coloring drawn in. I'm hoping you're stirred by this message, that you see that you are original, that there is a beautiful godliness in your ever-present originality, and that you should guard and protect this sacred source since it is what makes you feel alive and present here on earth. But I also don't want to spare you the scary part of the story. I want you to worry if you aren't finding ways to access your sacred originality and express it, and to see those places where you have failed to do so as dangerous, and to also locate where others and institutions might be holding it back.

Purple Crayons takes a sort of developmental approach to Harold, walking you through his stage-by-stage growth as a dignified human being. Since our dignity and originality are powerfully related, each stage I describe is also a small lesson on what it takes to allow our internal gyroscope to guide our lives. In this, it's a small and humble attempt to do what the transcendentalists did: draw a portrait of the kind of person you need to be to stay a person in these modern times.

I wrote my book to share Johnson's work with you, in the way we use the word *sharing* for telling a story or for passing along information. More important, however, I wanted to share it with you in the other sense of the word: as something I feel belongs to me that I now want to also belong to you. I hope you take it in this way, making it your own. If you can do that, *Harold and the Purple Crayon* may show you a way to live in the modern world that is lively and liberating. In fact, if you read it correctly, it may give you the paraffin instrument to do exactly that.

Just pick your own color. Purple's taken.

Chapter 1

BEGINNING

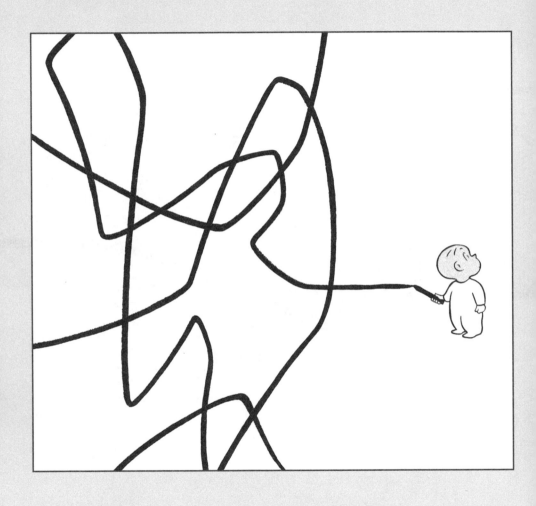

Harold and the Purple Crayon begins before the beginning, on a sort of prologue of a page before the title. Here we have our protagonist, paused in thought, surrounded by a scribble of purple lines he's drawn, which spreads past the page. Hand to chin, Harold surveys his work, maybe for the first time. He is still considering things when we turn to the first page, but he's now looking away from the squiggles and into blank space as he absentmindedly draws a straight line in the middle of that page. It's evening, and "after thinking it over for some time," Harold makes a decision: He wants to "go for a walk in the moonlight." There's one problem: There is no moon. So Harold draws one. With that act, the straight line now appears as a

horizon, and Harold's world instantly changes from one of squiggles to one of form. Living now in an illuminated world that makes sense, Harold draws a "long straight path" for his adventure.

Sound familiar? It's definitely a genesis, those first pages of *Harold and the Purple Crayon*, our hero emerging from an "earth without form" by letting "there be light." And what Harold does to transform a land of squiggles into solid terrain also matches the first moments of that other book: He starts dividing things.

"God saw the light, that it was good: and God divided the light from the darkness," and from here God goes into a scissor-spree of divisions: evening/morning, sky/land, earth/sea, and so on. God does this in order to give the world coherence, to have it make sense. Splitting everything up, God makes things recognizable by contrasting them. In this sense, "let there be light" means "let's name the darkness that came before all this," since you can only know darkness by introducing light, and you can only know light in its relationship to darkness. To put this more generally, the initial words of Genesis are about a certain rule in coherence: that things are only recognizable in relationship to things they are not. This rule is described well in those first poetic words of the Bible, but it's actually as down to earth as the mark of a dark purple crayon on a white page.

Let's look back at those first images of Harold and his emerging world. When Harold lifts his hand upward and above him, he severs the line drawn in the chaos of squiggles to create his first recognizable form. Once he draws that neat little crescent, its shape transforms the straight line into a horizon, the relationship between the two also transforming Harold's newest drawing into a moon. This image makes basic sense—the moon above, the horizon below, positioned in the way we think about moons and horizons—and it creates two more important things: an earth that ends at the horizon and the sky that begins where the earth ends.

Harold has created a lot here by simply drawing a semicircle above him, but the image still lacks depth, each object as close to our minds' eyes as Harold is. That all changes when Harold bends down in front of the line to draw the path. Once he does that, we see that he is in the foreground and the other two objects are in the background. His relationship to the line and the moon brings dimension to the picture, and with that there's closeness and distance, and now Harold can actually step on that path to explore.

Dividing, then relating to what is divided in order to create a world that is intelligible—it might be easy to mistake Harold's beginning as a remake of *In the Beginning*. But the first pages of *Harold and the Purple Crayon* aren't really about the genesis of earth, they're about the dawn of one coherent self—each crayoned form a little more detail in Harold's self-portrait.

Hit rewind and take away everything Harold draws, leaving only him on the page. Take away even the squiggle. For the sake of it, take away his crayon, too. He certainly stands out there—how could he not; after all, the page is otherwise blank. From looking at him there, we know a few things: that he's cute, he's clothed, and he doesn't seem in need of a haircut. But as Harold stands alone, we don't know much more than these superficial things. You'd think that just Harold there on the page, illustrated without the distraction or interference of other forms, would render him a completely discernible and identifiable human being—purely Harold.

But it doesn't, and that's why his crayon is everything.

Harold only becomes "real" because he draws other things in his environment that are decidedly *not* him. Harold alone is Harold, his one and only real talent being the ability to stand out on blank paper. When he begins to draw a world that he relates to, however, we begin to see the *Haroldness* in Harold, the *collection* of things that makes him unique. That, in turn, creates a story to be told.

Let's look at those things, and let's use the divide-and-relate rule to figure him out. There's actually a lot to discern in just a few pages, once Harold takes crayon to paper, most of it giving us a picture of how he relates to the world around him and thus to himself.

The first thing to notice about Harold is that he's fully drawn before the story begins. That creates a dramatic contrast between Harold and everything else on the page. Once we see that contrast, we also recognize that Harold exists somewhat independently of his world, since he's not born from it but *enters* into it. We don't know much about him so far, since he hasn't interacted with anything yet, but the fact that he's conceived before the story is a big piece of information and a big deal.

The second thing to notice is that Harold is the only figure in the story that is not purple. So he's made of different stuff than the other forms in his world, which are all made of the same stuff. As Harold is crayoned differently from everything around him, embarking on the story (rather than drawn by him into it) we can see that there is a sort of invisible boundary between what is Harold and what is not Harold.

That gets us to the third thing to notice, something that literally fills in some very important information about Harold's side of that boundary (which of course, in our new rule, fills in the other side, too). Look closely at Harold's head and hands: There's color inside the lines. And so, and unlike all the other drawings, Harold has an *inside*. That's a clue about an internal life, and that clue leads to a better understanding of what is on each side of that boundary: a perceiving and experiencing "me" of Harold that is separate from the purple "not me" on the other side, as the great psychoanalyst Donald Woods Winnicott would call it. Now we have Harold as his own individual person, with his own experiences, feelings, and thoughts, defined by how *separate* he is from the rest of the things in his environment, which don't (so far) experience, feel, or think. That changes everything.

Once we see Harold as sentient, he's no longer merely a figure we can detect as distinct by its relationship with other figures; he's having *relationships with them*. He's encountering them, engaging with them—doing things that objects can't do because, well, they're objects. The forms Harold draws are never going to see him, love him, or hate him, and so any encounter that Harold has with them is a one-way relationship.

Yet in that relationship, they do play a major part in Harold coming into form.

Take note: Other than the black silhouette and the shading of his skin, Harold is drawn with the same assured line and same simplicity and uniqueness of Johnson's hand as are all the other figures in the book. Johnson could have illustrated Harold in charcoal or paint, giving him shadow and depth; he could have pasted in a photo of a real boy; or he could have drawn Harold differently in the same medium, adding some crosshatching here, a thicker line there. But he didn't. That makes Harold one figure among many, his shape coming into distinct form in relationship to the others.

Harold's uniqueness in the world emerges from his relationship to things that are not him, independent of whether these things experience themselves in relationship with him. This is true for all of us.

To bring this point home, I encourage you to engage in a brief thought experiment here. It might feel a little self-helpy at first—like I'm asking you to do your daily affirmations—but it's absolutely not.

Here it is: Think of three things you like about yourself. Now stop and close your eyes for two minutes and think about these three things, maybe even come up with examples of how they manifest themselves in your life. I'll be here when you come back.

Ready to continue?

Now, I'm the furthest thing from clairvoyant, but I can confidently tell you something about each of the three things you picked, without knowing what they are: Every one of them connects you to the world, all incomplete without additional information about what or whom they relate to. If you picked "smart" or "curious" or "competent," you would need to answer *about or with what* for them to make sense, right? Or "kind" or "loving" or "gentle": *To whom?* Everything you do that makes you distinct is also the thing you do that *connects* you, and getting connected is also the thing that makes you distinct. (By the way, if I asked you what you hate about yourself, you would similarly need to answer with information about how your foibles disconnect you from others. Again, relationships.)

The next thing to notice in *Harold and the Purple Crayon* supports this point. Harold holds an object in his hand made from purple stuff, and he uses it to make more purple stuff. This information is important for two reasons—one a little obvious, the other not so much. First the obvious: Harold is the maker of the story, and all the purple objects are made. Harold is artistic in his approach to life, in other words. For more evidence on this fact, just look at him: We don't use crayons to write up contracts or sign checks; we use them for artistic enterprises.

Already, just a few pages in, we've seen what Harold does with that crayon and it's impressive: He draws a world and fills it with distinct things that are made distinct by their relationship to each other. While that may make Harold seem a little Godlike, it actually places him more squarely as someone being artistic. In fact, if you reduce it down, that is what art is all about: the human practice of dividing things, then seeing how they are related, then making something meaningful of this divide/relate process.

I mean, no offense to God, but the practice of creating a coherent picture by dividing light from dark, and then also parsing the gloaming and dawning mixtures of the two: that's basically illustrative arts 101—it's called a gray scale. This applies to art in general. Think about it: All storytelling—whether heard, read, or seen—is about relationships between separate beings, and we learn about the personalities of their characters by how they interact with each other and the world around them; in music the pauses are as important as the notes, and every chord is a relationship between notes; dance is about the relationship between movement and music, and/or dancer and dancer, and/or dancer and the space around her; and the visual arts are about the relationship between shadow and light, but *between* colors and *between* shapes.

We're really getting somewhere here. Looking at the images in

Harold and the Purple Crayon, it would be easy to conclude that the book is a sort of pamphlet selling the American dream: "Dream and it will happen!" "Anything is possible!" "Build it and they will come!" But considering Harold as artistic delivers a much more complex, deeper, and realistic revelation, a lesson on how to enter a relationship with the world in the same way artists do, but where the form you are sculpting is you.

To understand this more profound vision, you need to notice something many readers miss: The crayon is the only object other than Harold that is filled in, different from everything else on the page because it holds a sort of dual citizenship. In this way, it becomes Harold's intermediary to reach across the divide between him and what's outside him. His experiences, thoughts, and feelings, in other words, live on in the world of not-me, and the world of not-me also lives within his grip. He's not merely formed *from relationship*, his originality is expressed *in relationship*.

Now, let's face facts. Harold is able to do something most of us can't: draw recognizable things. But you absolutely don't have to be an Artist with a capital *A* to enter into a relationship in a creative way—far from it. Art imitates life; its processes are basic to our daily existence. When you make a good meal or eat one, kiss someone or are kissed, watch a sporting event or play a sport, work with colleagues, play with a child, or throw a party, you're given the opportunity to express who you are in the world of not-me. And the opposite is also true: The meal, the kiss, the sports, the collaborating, the playing, the partying are empty if you don't bring the me of your own original universe of thoughts, personality, and emotions with you—robotic behaviors without the corresponding filler of your inner life.

For Harold, and for all of us, there is an inside existence—a site of experience that we call a soul or a self—and there is an outside world that goes on whether we experience it or not. There is also a space between the inside of our experiences and the outside world called *relationship*. We all experience our original being—the way we color and texture our inner life—in that in-between space both by welcoming the outer world into our heads and hearts, and also by planting ourselves in that outer world by illustrating what's going on inside. The trick in all of this is our willingness to live *relatedly* as much as we can—to travel within the borderland between purple and not-purple, me and not-me.

We now arrive at our final look at Harold on these first pages. Once Harold lays out a horizon, every object he creates, other than the moon, exists on earth, and it's from earth where things sprout and grow (which they do for Harold in the next pages). This gets us to why I think human originality is sacred. When you can make it to the middle path of relationship, something marvelous, even magical, occurs: You feel alive and you experience the world around you as alive, too. Our purple crayons are soul stirrers, in this sense, conjuring in us an experience that I call *livingness*—the sense of life coursing through us and through the things we encounter. I'll describe this idea in more detail in the pages to come, but for now look at that child on the page: What is he doing throughout the book? It's obvious: He's animating a world in which he grows.

Less obvious is the fact that he's also fighting to keep his livingness alive. That's not easy for any of us.

Here is why, and it has to do with something that's a little chicken-and-egg. True: Things are made distinct in relationship to other things and beings. And: A relationship is something that only occurs between things that are distinct. Like a purple crayon drawn by a purple crayon, you have to start somewhere. Artists try to outsmart this paradox by drawing figures and their relationship to other figures at the same time, their eyes dancing between the emerging forms and the shape and form of the negative space between them. Harold's creator, of course, does this more assertively: He just plops a fully drawn figure of a boy onto the page.

Easy for Johnson, but maybe not for Harold. Left there on his own, Harold now has to take the risk of adding something of himself to a world that is not yet formed and marked by uncertainty. He has to "put it out there," as we appropriately say. And that makes behaving on the basis of his own original feelings, thoughts, and intuition difficult.

When you contribute something of your own inner life to the world of others, it's like an artist adding their first strokes to the painting. You really don't know precisely how things will turn out as you first try to articulate something and before it's fully realized through relationship. "What if I can't even make it clear?" "What if it's ugly?" "What if people hate it?" And so, "What if the things that most make me, me are unseen by others or seen as ugly or despicable?" That's risky. You're also going to face something else that is upsetting: Nothing will happen for you that has any sense of life to it unless you take the risk to draw. For these two reasons—the uncertainty of it all and the worry about your accountability as the drafter of your life—we very often resist being original and thus live outside of a related approach to the world, subsisting instead of living, our presence much like figures on a canvas someone else has drawn.

At least that has been my experience the past sixty years. On any given day, there are points in which my own unique inner being engages with another—in conversation, collaboration, sharing a meal, and so forth. At these moments there's an experience of encountering me and not-me, and the space between the two. It's all there when it happens: a self that is distinct and alive—multiplied by division. It's so profoundly meaningful, these moments of *Rossness*, close to what we call fulfillment, I think. And it's free, right there for the taking.

It's also fleeting. I feel lucky when I get there. On a given day, and often without notice, my sense of inner continuity is regularly disturbed by something—a difficult interaction with someone at work, a friend's slight, a child's anger, someone's criticism, my own self-doubt, a tweet—and I lose a sense of my internal consistency, feeling anxious, disturbed, or, worse in some ways, empty of any feeling. I have the experience in these moments of "disintegrating," as psychologists call it, my *Rossness* becoming like a tab of Alka-Seltzer dropped in water. In these moments I clamber to get back to some sense of a continuous me. But I don't always make the best choices as I try to get back. Often as I'm clambering to get back to myself, I want to feel so integrated, so solid and impenetrable, that I begin to behave in black-or-white terms. At these moments, I stop trying to be related to the world but choose a side in the division between myself and the things and beings that are not-me—a split between "individuation and merger" as psychologists call these sides. In some cases, I might lean toward being separate but not related, becoming either egotistical—a fully in charge Master of my Universe—or totally insecure, believing I don't deserve contact with a world that goes on without me. Other times I go in the opposite direction, seeing the world outside me as a welcomed guide to my existence. In this situation, I might try harder to appease others, to blend in as much as possible, to ingratiate in order to integrate. Here again, I don't really feel like myself (clearly: I just conformed!) Both of these routes I take work rather well in calming my sense that I'm disintegrating. But there's a toll at each road; I must forfeit my uniqueness as a creating human being.

As you'll see, Harold experiences the same sorts of disintegrating moments, and the ways he picks himself up are often a master class in how to recover in the deepest and most dignified way possible. (Hint: He continues to draw.) But along the way Harold often makes the same mistakes in his recovery that I do in mine; he splits between isolating or complying in ways I'm guessing you also can recognize in your own life. The deadening consequence of these mistakes is graphically depicted late in the book, when Harold loses his grip, the crayon gone from his hand.

It's difficult and risky to bring your own impulses, imagination, and wants and needs to the table, especially when much more secure options are available in a more risk-averse way. I'll illustrate this in more detail up ahead, and I'll also show how this problem of staying cohesively creative isn't just a matter of art but something that involves our brain, the most human part of it built to be in relationship through our originality, while the lizard part runs like hell from negative space when things feel dangerous. For now, it's important you understand that expressing your own originality is very much worth it, but that it's something that's also very scary to do.

It's worth it because it's the thing that stirs our souls and allows us to feel and experience the aliveness of the world around us (yes, genesis-like, again). It's scary because of all that risk of disintegration and deadness.

It's hard to take that risk without some sense of security around us, some trust that we can return to our path if things go wrong when we leave it. That's why originality has its own discerning relationship. To do the creative thing, we need to feel there's something not very creative within our reach, something durable, that doesn't change too much, that goes on without us and shows up exactly when and where we know it will.

Something moonlike.

When Harold reaches his hand up at the very beginning of the book, the crayon ending a mark born in chaos and then marking the page again to draw something neat and concise, he creates the only object that both sticks with him throughout the story, and repeatedly returns without Harold drawing it.

As you well know by now, he couldn't have illustrated anything else without that moon.

Chapter 2

HOLDING

The moon sits steadily in the sky, ready to follow Harold wherever he goes, its light blanketing a landscape that reaches all the way to the horizon. Under its vast illumination, Harold is confident he won't get lost as he travels, so he heads out, taking the maiden steps of his journey.

Harold is walking into a lot of uncertainty here, an unknowable world he won't know until he reaches out and draws it. He's doing the yeoman's work of independence, creating the path that he then walks

on. But he's not really alone in this challenge since he has that moon, its reliable beam providing him enough security to take the risk.

Look at the first image opposite, the one with Harold looking over his shoulder. Now place your thumb over the moon. What do you make of Harold standing on that path? Does he look a little lonely to you? Do you worry about him? To me, he seems quite helpless, unprotected, and even in danger, an expression of anxiety on his face. As I look at the image, the moon now obstructed by my thumb, I'm not sure he's going to head out on his journey. He may stay put on the path, averting risk. Now remove your thumb from the moon. How does Harold look? He appears to me like he's preparing to depart, sort of figuring things out as he emerges from a world of squiggles to a world of forms. He's calm enough to afford being quizzical, pondering his next move, yet also energized and eager to get going, his expression one of anticipation.

If we want to venture out into the world we draw, we need the experience Harold has here with the moon: the sense of something in our lives that is dependably secure. Psychologists call this experience "holding."

Found in parents, family, friends, and more abstract things like shared beliefs, religion, and culture, holding is the sense of security gained by being physically held but with no arms physically wrapped around you. It's the psychological feeling of something solidly comforting and protective, guarding you from forces outside the parameter of you and from those inside you, too—those urges that push you to cross dangerous lines that you shouldn't.

When we know there is something or someone in our life that we can rely on, we're given enough security to roam freely. The opposite is also true: When all around us is only squiggled chaos, we're lonely in a crowd, insecure and afraid, even when we're in close physical proximity to other people. With a giant thumb covering our moon, we're lost.

Like Harold and his moon, good holding doesn't clamp us in place; it's portable—the "long straight path" on which we autonomously improvise. This seeming paradox is in fact the rule for all acts of creativity: Your willingness to draw what you want is directly related to how much you feel contained by something assuredly real that exists independent of your creative impulses. "Be regular and orderly in your life, so that you may be violent and original in your work," wrote the great French novelist Gustave Flaubert. Or as the jazz musician Branford Marsalis puts it: "You don't play what you feel. There's only freedom in structure." Both are completely right, and not just about stories and jazz but about any creative approach to living.

Winnicott had a really good term for the experience of holding that describes its paradoxical nature as something that contains us to make us free: "to be alone in the presence of another." To feel held is to have an adventure on your own under the watchful eye of a caring and reliable source.

Harold's moon provides its young charge with the kind of container we all need in order to be free, but it's not quite separate from him, since it's born from his hand, and it's this kind of in-between experience that Winnicott is implying. Imagine the book beginning with the moon on the very first page, just like Harold is plopped there by Johnson. It would now appear a little like a sidekick, and a different title for the book enters my head: *Harold and the Moon*, with the crayon taking a backseat to Harold and his friend. Sure, the moon in this new version may protect Harold and may provide light for his journey, but it's more of a collaborator with Harold, lending a hand at all times in the design of a world they both roam, rather than providing the illumination for a trek that only Harold is on. Johnson makes an ingenious move by having Harold create his source of security. This captures something very important about how holding works and is connected to our willingness to create. You see, holding really isn't a one-way event, in which you are the passive recipient of a good hug, but more of a mutual embrace. In other words, we need to put something into holding to get something out of it. And that mutuality begins at a young age.

When children emerge into selves—dividing from the world in order to relate to it—they experience their caretakers as partly conjured by their own powers. This feeling that they've birthed those caretakers creates a confidence to explore the world: The child's ability to feel alone, yet still safe, depends on a repeated mental summoning of their caretaker's embrace. It's a magical thing, what children do: They turn their caretakers into "introjects," as psychologists call them.

When they are lucky, these introjects become sources of security that the little one can cart around even when the caretaker is no longer in close physical proximity. When they are unlucky, the opposite is true: The child doesn't trust the world that goes on without them, and so they don't metabolize the things a comforting other may provide, even when it's provided with a lot of warmth and security. (Yes, thumbs over moons.)

As lucky children turn into lucky adults, they walk farther and farther away from the physical site of the holding yet are still able to experience it as a source that is always there. Soon they find other sources for feeling held, their moon now a composite of many different holders, some identifiable (friends, coworkers, extended family, therapists) and some part of a larger patchwork in the social fabric (religion and cultural enterprises being the most important examples).

As far as identified holders, social psychologists have a term for how we adults populate our consciousnesses with a sort of team of individuals we mentally cart around, some of whom we are deeply connected to emotionally, others less so: "perceived social support." Think about your own team, the people who cheer you on and are there for you if things don't work out—friends, family, coworkers are all examples. Perceived social support is how you experience this team regardless of how much cheering and protection you're actually receiving at a given moment. Research on perceived social support shows that these people don't have to be in the room with you when you need them: Just by imagining them and thinking about them "being there" for you, you reap the benefits of their support. Those benefits are significant: higher self-esteem, a greater sense of your own competence, lower depression and anxiety, and better physical health. Such perception also affects how we experience threats and challenges independently of how much actual social support we have at the moment. Indeed, when subjects in experiments merely think about a time when they felt they were not socially supported, they perceive threats as more threatening and challenges as more challenging than do subjects who first recollect a moment when they were supported.

That's one important thing that makes lucky adults, adults, and all children, children: Unlike childhood, adulthood is marked by the ability to play the long game in the magic of holding, to depend more on our own invocations of perceived support than on the regular reassurance of a nearby caregiver. Since we can take care of ourselves, we don't need constant proof that we are protected. Or, to put it another way, because we no longer need this proof—we're able to bring our team along for the ride—we feel protected enough to depend on ourselves.

In this light, Harold is more adult, or more readily tapping into his inner adult, than most children's book protagonists. The moon's ability to hold Harold depends mostly on his own conjuring abilities; whereas other characters—Max in *Where the Wild Things Are*, or the bunny in *The Runaway Bunny*, for example—depend on the reassuring realness of nearby caretakers to feel safe. That's a really important difference. It's also one of two things that make Harold's relationship with the moon stand out.

While the moon is made *by Harold*, it doesn't belong *to him*, since moons are things other people walk beneath. Thus, Harold has no exclusive rights to his source of holding. This, again, makes Harold more adultlike and less like a lot of children's book characters: think Curious George and the Man with the Yellow Hat, or Dorothy Gale's team of social supporters in *The Wonderful Wizard of Oz*.

As we become adults, we find a sense of holding in more generalized forms, no longer completely dependent on identifiable figures like parents or even specific social supports but on something more universal. Throughout history, religious deities (God, gods, and holy beings) have been the clearest embodiment of this experience, ubiquitous forces that mind us and animate our souls. It's no surprise that early religions tended to see divinity in the sun, a celestial object that made the world safe through illumination, warmth, and—the occasional eclipse aside—dependability.

So imagine Harold walking under that moon, in a landscape where there are also others walking, all bathing in its light as an enduringly watchful source, and then picture these individuals gathering once a week to support each other in the belief that the moon is well worth sanctifying, and you get a bit of a picture of how religion works as a shared source of holding. In this view, religion is the institution where we celebrate what bonds us, where we keep bonding, and where we experience this bond as something a little beyond us—something we tap into rather than just create.

Religion always provides a sense of being held by a higher power (even in the valley of the shadow of death, "thou art with me"). In fact, that may be one big reason for its existence—or, depending on where you come down on such things, why we invented it. According to the great sociologist Émile Durkheim, religion is "an eminently collective thing," a means for people to experience the whole as greater than the parts of our connections through shared symbols, stories, customs, and traditions. In this admittedly secular view, the function of religion is to gather into one comprehensible entity all the spaces of relationships between us in order to provide a shared sense of something enduringly mindful that exists *outside* us. This gathering lets us further connect, as we face the same way and see the same thing, practice the same rituals and tell the same stories under the same pitched, domed, tiled, thatched, or starry roof.

Religion is an eminently cultural thing, too, expressed through stories, art, music, and architecture. In fact, one way to rethink Durkheim's view of religion is as a means by which culture is contained and made familiar, a physical or metaphysical site where you can be assured that you're looking at the same moon as the other parishioners. That doesn't have to happen in a temple. Speak the same language, use the same symbols, employ the same gestures, tell the same jokes and stories, engage in games handed down through generations, dance at a house party or in a club, make crafts your parents once made, play a sport, be a sports fan, read a book, cook from a recipe, look at art, talk about a movie, love your country—all these things offer the opportunity to experience a sense of a social bond that is greater than you.

Well before Harold, in the Western world religion had loosened its grip on the monopoly of overarching holding, and in the United States especially we were also losing the sense of a predictable world of customs and traditions in general, wiped away in large part by industrialization. And in the 1950s, we were seeing a growing trend toward what would fill the void left by this: style, brand, buying the things your neighbor has—outer-focused behaviors, as the authors of *The Lonely Crowd* would call them. To be the same as everyone else was a means to feel like you were on the inside, safe and protected.

In many ways, we live today in the world that Johnson and others of his time were worried about. Many thinkers back then were concerned about the commodification of everything, including ourselves, all of it available for the right price. In this environment, holding becomes something you purchase, the things you own or pay to do replacing traditions as a means to feel connected to something bigger than yourself. (And buy and own we did and do: At the time of Erich Fromm's famous book on commodification, *To Have or to Be?*, there were no storage units for all the extra stuff someone had purchased. Today, there are approximately two billion square feet of them in the United States.)

Much of this has been driven by the culture industry—a mass

appropriation of what were once the products of artisans and artists for commercial purposes. Put down your crayon for a moment and look around. How often do the products you purchase promise you a sense of comforting solidity? Think about the word *artisanal*, for example. When you think about it, does it conjure up images of unique products made by humans when they are at their most original, or do you think about things like Wendy's Artisan Egg Sandwich, the Artisan Bagels at Dunkin' Donuts, Weight Watchers Artisan Creations? In such cases (and there are thousands more), the terms *artisanal* or *artisan*—and likewise terms such as *handcrafted*, *small batch*, and *homemade*—are simply a slapped-on label to take advantage of our wish to be held within homespun communities.

One more example of this packaged promise of holding is the Super Bowl, which has evolved in American culture from a relatively modest professional championship to the biggest sporting event in the country. A big part of its growth is about consumerism and branding, with fans going from wearing regular clothes to T-shirts with a team's name or an image of its quarterback to wildly expensive replica jerseys and halftime shows becoming garish productions meant (quite patronizingly) to attract women to the audience. Most tellingly, the Super Bowl broadcast has become so much about the commercials produced specifically for it that some people just watch them online and ignore the event itself. And don't forget the name of the stadiums: "Bank this," "Bank that." Was football ever "pure"?

Of course not. But we're now at a state where your fandom is authenticated by how much gear you own, and the game itself is both promoted and demoted by Bud Light and Geico. When we sit down on that Sunday and watch the Super Bowl, we feel a deep sense of connectedness to all the other viewers. That connectedness is as real as any moment in which shared symbols and meanings bring us together, but at this point it's fundamentally manufactured to get us to buy stuff. To put it blatantly, it's a radical commodification of our traditional social bond, a way to make money off our need to feel held by some sense of commonness that is greater than any one of us.

And here's the profoundly important problem with the purchasing of your psychological security: While the goods you buy may give you some sense of being part of things, you are joining a club that only survives by convincing you to chronically shed what you already have and buy something new to replace it. Newness and change drive the constant selling around us, seducing you to consume not just more of the products you already have consumed but new or better ones, too. Thus the constant change in the symbols and trends we share, every one of them a notice that you no longer fit in and a promise of how you can take care of that. It's really a magnificently efficient one-two punch that hits us with great precision and speed: First, there's a void in your being that, left unfilled, will make you unacceptable to others, threatening any chance to be part of a holding community, and second, lucky for you, companies offer a corresponding commodity that will fill the void. That's not a very safe and dependable way to live, in a world of rapidly changing outer forces. In fact, it's just the opposite.

"We find it more and more difficult to achieve a sense of continuity, permanence, or connection with the world around us," wrote Christopher Lasch more than four decades ago. "Relationships with others are notably fragile; goods are made to be used up and discarded; reality is experienced as an unstable environment of flickering images." Today, more than ever, the world outside our skulls is at best an unreliable site for the holding we need to be our original selves—and chaotically invasive at worst. The result of this is a lot of insecurity.

"Just when we are in many ways moving to an ever greater validation of the sacredness of the individual person," wrote the sociologist Robert Bellah, "our capacity to imagine a social fabric that would hold individuals together is vanishing." This is due in large part to commercialism. In other words, we have this amazing gift in our hands if only we have the right opportunities to hold it: that modern promise of an originally drawn life. But this opportunity is the result of a void that was then filled for profit.

Now, with all this writing about the doom and gloom of a capitalism in overdrive, let's not forget that *Harold and the Purple Crayon* is basically a celebration of the gift part of the modern scenario. Just look at Harold as he sets out—the anxious expectancy, the sense of risk, the noticeable joy as he prepares to encounter a world. It's just that Harold can't really enjoy what's promised him without courageously overcoming modern psychological threats. The modern gift, in this sense, is something taken, not just given.

To unwrap the gift of sacred originality and to protect ourselves from the threat of a world that wants nothing more than for us to conform, we must rely on ourselves more than at any other time to find our holding, to summon it as much as possible, and to reach out and make it happen: with our social supports, with our religion, with our culture, with our political involvement, and in our neighborhoods. If we want to feel held we have to put more in than our ancestors did, to get anything out—to be Harolds.

And what Harold does next in relationship to that moon is a lesson for us adults on what we need to do in order for our lives to be meaningful in this place and time. Held in the blanket of moonlight, Harold does what comes naturally to all children when they feel secure: He goes out to play.

Chapter 3

PLAYING

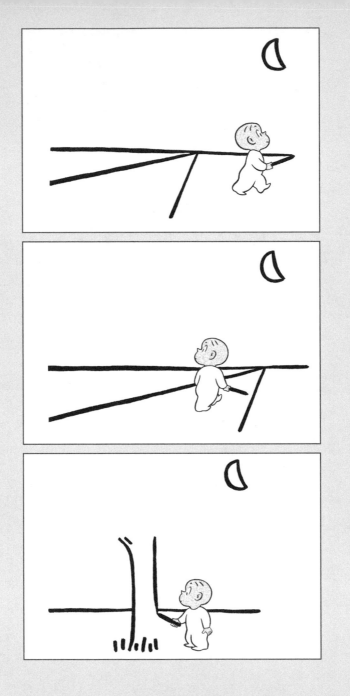

Harold doesn't go far on the "long straight path"— just a few initial steps, and he feels like he's not "getting anywhere." So with the moon watching over him, he decides to leave the fixed route "for a short cut across a field," to a place where he thinks "a forest ought to be." Harold is letting his impulses and intuition guide him, the sturdiness of the moon giving him the security to veer off course. The route ahead is no longer laid out in front of him. Instead, it reaches only to the point where the crayon leaves its newest mark. Harold's playing with what's next.

To play is to first see the pliability of things—to regard objects, ways of thinking, and other beings that can seem unyielding and solid as actually malleable—and second, to make them partly your own, material with which to express your originality. When you play, you are stepping into the unknown, since you can't know what's ahead until you create it.

Think of a child playing with her toys. We've already established that she experiences herself as almost magical, having conjured her parent there, minding her while she plays. That magic doesn't stop at the holding other, however. In fact, the sense of security gained by her ability to hold her caregivers in her mind gives her the ability to do another magical thing: conjure life into inanimate objects. That's mostly what childhood play is all about, toys becoming things with life (from a talking candlestick to a depressed stuffed donkey, it's also a central component of children's literature). In this sense, the child's magic is twofold: She experiences herself as drawing the world of purple that exists outside of her (that holding space of consistency) while at the same time she welcomes the world of purple into the home that is her, animating it in her mind. In giving life to her toys, she is preparing herself to find that middle space of relatedness I described in chapter one: the area between a reality that exists independent of her and her own original existence.

"It is in playing and only in playing," according to Winnicott, "that the individual child or adult is able to be creative and to use the whole personality, and it is only in being creative that the individual discovers the self." In play, we are not only clearing the "dust of everyday life," as the jazz drummer and bandleader Art Blakey put it, but also "cleaning the mirror" that shows who we are, as the saxophone genius John Coltrane said when he described playing jazz. And jazz does teach us a lot about play.

There's an interesting experiment about original me-ness in play done by Charles Limb and Allen Braun, two doctors at Johns Hopkins University. Their research consists of studying images of the brains of jazz musicians and freestyle rappers while they improvise.

Turns out that the medial prefrontal cortex—the part of the brain linked to self-expression and conveying originality—lights up during improvisation. It's the same part of the brain that also lights up when you tell a story about yourself.

I bet you know what it's like to be fully engaged in telling a story about yourself to people who are fully engaged with what you have to say. If you reflect on how it feels—the sense of shared vivacity—you can get a sense of how play brings things to life. In these moments, you're using shared language, common metaphors, and maybe even a classic story structure to express something about yourself. There's you, using the world outside you, to say something original about you: again, that middle space between me and not-me, that border between the non-purple Harold and the purple land he draws with an instrument that he possesses. Of course, reading a story also brings you to that purple/not-purple borderland, your mind collaborating with the author as you experience the characters as alive, and feeling a sense of inner aliveness as you read. As I mentioned, I call this experience *livingness*, by which I mean the experience rather than the knowledge of your aliveness: the vibrational sense that you live and are among other living things and beings.

"When you are playing . . . there's one thing that remains constant," said Coltrane. "And that is the tension of the experience, that electricity, that kind of feeling that is a lift sort of feeling. No matter where it happens, you know when that feeling comes upon you, and it makes you feel happy." The tension between forces, the relationship and the electricity that come from this tension: Coltrane has precisely described the livingness that comes from play.

There's always a wild component to play, a push against the hard earth in order to feel alive. If the initial pages of Harold's story play with the first sentences of Genesis—art transforming nothing into something—these new pages invert the story of Adam, with Harold not banished from paradise but banishing an orderly world to eagerly strike out into the wilds of fields and forests. When we don't play, it is to do the opposite—to be domesticated, not wild, to live a *Groundhog Day* existence, in which the first light of morning is only a rote reminder of lifeless living.

That makes play serious business. Sometimes deeply so. In his book *Prisoner Without a Name, Cell Without a Number*, the Jewish Argentinean journalist Jacobo Timerman describes his imprisonment in Argentina during the Dirty War, where thousands were "disappeared." Alone in his cell, forbidden from communicating, he was terrified. There was a slit in his steel door through which he could see only the steel door opposite his with its slit. Once, looking out, he saw the eyes of another prisoner looking back at him. The eyes were there, then not there, then there, then not there. The fellow prisoner was playing the simplest game, something close to peekaboo. Timerman describes this moment of play, in which his fellow inmate made something innovative out of something so oppressively fixed, as a central preserving force during the first, most terrifying days in prison. There's a good chance that Timerman would have survived physically without the game of peekaboo. But playing kept his selfhood alive.

Imagine if Harold had never cut across that field, remaining throughout the book on his original path. That story might be one about staying playful despite restrictions, or it might be about what it means to be a good boy, someone who never breaks the rules, and walks directly home from school. It could also be a book about emptiness and boredom, a life without any use for purple crayons, raising important questions about the threat of a playless life. But Johnson didn't want to write that book, and that's what makes *Harold and the Purple Crayon* a sort of warning about a playless, and thus lifeless, life.

"All I could see was a lot of bright young men in gray flannel suits rushing around New York in a frantic parade to nowhere," says the protagonist in Sloan Wilson's 1955 novel, *The Man in the Gray Flannel Suit*. "They seemed to me to be pursuing neither ideals nor happiness—they were pursuing a routine. For a long while I thought I was on the sidelines watching that parade, and it was quite a shock to glance down and see that I, too, was wearing a gray flannel suit." To exist without play is to approach life as unchangeable by you, and to exist without a core—to live "one-dimensionally," as the Frankfurt School sociologist Herbert Marcuse describes it. Others have had similar insight about the pitfalls of living with a "spirit of serious-ness," as the existential philosopher Jean-Paul Sartre called it: to operate without originality or agency; to be a product or consumer, never a producer or creator.

We are not the only animals who play, but the reason for our play is unique to us. Humans are distinguished from other animals by the fact that we collaborate with others of our kind in order to invent. And regardless of whether others are actually in the room with us when we collaborate, we're always relying on the material created by people who are not present—purple crayons, for example. And it's this back-and-forth, between our inner lives and an outer world—this constant crossing between the land of not-purple and the purple world—that makes us cultural.

"I feel that jazz improvisation is the ultimate," says the saxophonist Sonny Rollins. "You have to create on the spot, the essence of this music." Take apart that last sentence and you locate a central paradox of jazz, and of play in general. Any jazz musician will tell you that when they're improvising, they're doing so in conversation not only with their bandmates but with the essence of the music itself—the ancient sediment of chords, chord progressions, time signatures, and music theory (a part of that structure that allows for freedom, as Branford Marsalis put it in the previous chapter). To play is to always play *with* something, even if it's just an idea in your head. Or, to quote Rollins again: "Everyone is derivative."

He is right: Nothing we play with comes from thin air since there's culture in the clay of every original act. Even when we break from an old way of doing something, we're playing with it. The word *innovate* means to do something we've already done in a new way, a gentle reminder from our ancestors that we walk on roads they paved. We rely on an outer world that exists of its own accord and carries with it familiar symbols and customs we can connect with, material we use for invention. In this way, culture doesn't just hold us in a manner that allows us to be spontaneous; it provides the material we have to do so. It's the caretaker in whose presence we play, and it's the toys we play with, too.

"It is not possible to be original except on a basis of tradition," wrote Winnicott. This is also true in reverse: It's not possible to truly feel the life of an outer world without bringing our originality to the table. Think, for a moment, about listening to your favorite song. Isn't there a *you* that's made more vibrant when you relate to that song? Isn't there also an experience of a relationship between you and not-you that feels more universal—a sense of "all music"? Isn't that one reason you love a particular song—that it makes you feel connected to something bigger than you?

While you may have had nothing to do with the creation of this cherished song, what you gain from listening to it is tremendously dependent on your own originality: You chose the song, the song means something to you, it reflects your particular tastes in music, and it might also be your favorite because it resonates so powerfully with your own memories and experiences. In fact, it's nothing to you without your collaboration.

To play is to enter an "original relation to the universe," in Emerson's words; to conjure our own connection with something bigger than us by acting on our own unique impulses, tastes, and talents. And this kind of original relationship is dormant in every book, painting, sculpture, film, play, and song, ready to present itself as long as we're willing to animate it.

As that child described above invents a life for her toys, she's preparing to become an adult who continues to create an "original relation to the universe" in all kinds of ways, most neither identifiably artistic nor existing in some sort of fantasy land. And when we are given the opportunity to do that, we're in touch with that collaborating/inventing gene in all humans, and thus we are in touch with our humanity. Karl Marx called this our "species essence."

Yes, Karl Marx. If that name worries you, take a big breath and read on. I know Marx is a big turnoff for a lot of people today, mostly because when they hear his name they think only of the brutal authoritarian governments that claimed to follow his economic and political theories, and which violently forced uniform lifestyles on people. But, in fact, Marx had a lot of brilliant things to say about what it is that makes us most human, ideas that were very important in Johnson's time, species essence being one of them.

To understand this concept, think of a bird: A bird's species essence—its *birdness*—is expressed and experienced in flight; it is most a bird when it is flying. The tragedy of a caged bird is the limiting of its freedom, but the main reason this restriction is tragic is because it limits the bird's *birdness*—the fact that it can't do what birds are meant to do. For Marx, our humanness is expressed and experienced when we are free to take in the world outside us, make something creative out of it, then place it back in that world (yes, middling between me/not-me, purple/not-purple).

Think about that for a second, and maybe add a little of what you learned in your high-school bio class: All living things do what Marx sees as integral to reaching our essence, but in a biological way, ingesting something from their environment, metabolizing it, then returning it to the world in a new and fertile form. Pardon the scatology of that metaphor, but it's important, since it places our livingness very close to something we naturally do. That electricity Coltrane refers to? We now see its source: It is us, when we are being as human as we can be, by doing what comes naturally: playing.

Marx still turning you off? Here's another way to look at this that has religious overtones: At the time of Harold's birth, several modern theologians were taking a good hard look at how much God and Émile Durkheim's "eminently collective thing" might be one and the same. In this view, we don't go to places of worship to revere what's really just a social bond: The social bond *is* God. For Martin

Buber and Paul Tillich, God was something that happens in dialogue not only with an outer divine presence but between us and the world around us. They believed in a God that was not a specific thing but was conjured up in the in-between of us and a world outside us. Buber called the relationship we create when we live in a dialogue with the world an "I-Thou" one.

"All real living is meeting," wrote Buber, and what he meant by this is that we feel most alive in our humanity when our me engages with an outer not-me. But it's not just us alone in these moments of dialogue: We also have an experience of the Thou—the holy place of connection. Thus, as I already mentioned, Buber agrees with Durkheim that *religion* is an "eminently collective thing" but he puts God back into the mix, "God" being that "collective thing."

Whether you side with Marx or with modern theologians like Buber, or with both (many of latter had little beef with a lot of former, by the way), I think you can see the tragedy that happens when we can't play. Whether due to political oppression, psychological insecurity, or something else, playlessness—Sartre's "spirit of seriousness"—means losing touch with the essence of our humanity. This is the tragedy of what Marx called *alienation*, the severing of our deepest humanity from what we do; an estrangement of our species essence that makes us experience our "own body, external nature . . . mental life, and . . . human life" as alien. It's what Buber called an "I-It" relationship, in which we experience the world outside us as lifeless, and hence experience less life inside ourselves.

It's Marx's concern about alienation that most ties Harold (who, to borrow yet another term from Marx, controls a purple "means of production" in his hand) to Johnson's early drawings for *New Masses* and publications of a similar bent, one of them even showing a sort of Harold prototype, a little boy holding a protest flag. Harold's predecessors and contemporaries fought directly against the forces of alienation. By choosing an improvisational route, Harold's showing us the richness and value and sheer human essence in play, and he's fighting against the onslaught of anti-play forces.

Harold was conceived at a moment in history when play was under threat within the larger American culture, very much com-modified into salable amusements. Disney, television, and the dangerous congealing of commerce and mass uniformity: These forces promised entertainment and material abundance beyond anything that had come before, but in reality, they were *play-destroying* by commodifying play into something that was bought and sold, an activity that was unyielding and inaccessible to the individual's creative contribution. In the 1950s, genuine, spontaneous play was increasingly replaced by things to consume, or by working hard in order to afford them.

But as the forces of consumerism threatened to consume *us*, Harold allies himself with the resistance: with the beboppers and

jazz masters; with the beats, the folk revivalists, and modern danc-
ers; the rock and rollers, the critical theorists, the existentialists, the
Mattachinists, the absurdists, the pop artists, the liberal theologians,
the foul-mouthed comedians, and anyone else in the era of *Harold
and the Purple Crayon*'s publication who not only stood in defiance
of conformity but pushed against it. Harold and his cadre were
fighting for the liveliness in their—and our—lives (the Cat in the
Hat joining in, with his version of disobedient, anarchic play). And
in this, they were fighting for the thing that makes us most human.

And in *that*, they were fighting for another important and very
human faculty, something very much like play, that makes play fea-
sible but is not quite play.

Watch a jazz musician improvise. Their eyes are almost always
shut. That's because they are in a kind of dream state, in which they
put all kinds of disparate notes and sounds together to articulate
something original. Think of freestyle rappers—the other subjects in
Charles Limb and Allen Braun's study—who also tend to keep their
eyes shut as they combine words to make rhymes and stories. Both
are very much inside their brains, assembling material from outside
them in order to express themselves.

Part of the genius of improvising musicians and rappers is that
they can do what they do at such a rapid-fire pace. That genius can
also conceal the process they are engaged in, since what they are
doing is something we often associate with ponderous daydreaming:

They are imagining. Imagination is what Harold uses when he takes material from the land of purple to welcome it into his brain so he can innovate with it. And when Harold cuts that path across the field, he's letting his imagination roam. His pace may be a bit more leisurely than Coltrane at his most liberated, but Harold is also off to the races.

Chapter 4

IMAGINING

arold doesn't wander haphazardly when he takes his playful journey off the beaten path. Instead— and for the first time—his gaze looks beyond the mark of his crayon to a destination he envisions is just up ahead, that place where "a forest ought to be." Once Harold arrives there, ready to draw, he worries that he'll get lost if the forest is too big, so he sketches the smallest forest possible: a single tree that is full of apples. Looking up, Harold fancies that the apples will be red when ripe and "very tasty" once they're ready to eat.

Everything that Harold senses on these pages exists beyond his drawing—it's in a land of what's next, what's around the corner.

He's imagining, combining distinct things into wholes: a path with a forest edge; the size of the forest with the fear of getting lost; apples in a tree and what they will taste like when they're ready.

And here's another example of how we all are artistic, even if we don't think of ourselves as artists. Imagination is a kind of artist's studio in your head for trying out many kinds of combinations of distinct and often disparate-seeming things and assembling them into something new. Right now, for example, I'm looking at that image of the apple tree, and I'm thinking about the Garden of Eden. That often comes to mind when I see a rendering of apple trees, but also because the tree is the first living thing Harold draws, and I'm thinking about the creation of life and also about what it means to strike out on your own. That's got me wondering, too, whether anything similar was going on in Johnson's head when he placed an apple tree in the book so close to the beginning.

While all this is going on in my brain, it's not exactly the product of thinking in terms of reaching a rational decision, as it is a gathering of distinct images and concepts that are initially related only in that they all popped into my head at that moment. In this case, in addition to the Garden of Eden's tree of knowledge, a regular apple tree, a forest, and Johnson, there's a Peter Paul Rubens painting, and several other images floating in a sort of blank space in my mind's eye. Without me quite trying, a few of these images then came together, and I imagined a baroque painting of Harold in

Eden. Neurologists call the complex neural network that allowed me to do all this a "mental workspace."

You imagine life in this workspace.

That's quite a dramatic thing to say, but here is what I mean: Whether it's the life in you, something inanimate you bring to life, or another living being, you can't actually see that vivacity in anything—you can only imagine it. Or, to put it another way, you go to your mental workspace to forge aliveness in the things, ideas, and beings around you. That's what Harold's doing when he looks at the apples and imagines them as red. It's also what the child is doing when she imagines her toy as alive, and what adults do when they are able to feel compassion or empathy for other living things. In all these endeavors, imagination is their means to encountering the life in something outside them.

The anthropologist Gregory Bateson is really helpful here in understanding the connection between imagination and perceiving the livingness in the world around us. As he explained, nature—the land of living things—is always ecological: No one thing can be understood as standing alone, because everything is interconnected. Bateson used a term for this world of living things that he borrowed from Carl Jung: "creatura."

Creatura is filled with distinct *forms* of life, made distinc*tive* by their relationship to other distinct forms. You can't grasp the livingness in these forms without seeing the space between them. That's because life doesn't exist only inside life-forms; it's formed by their relationships, since they are interdependent.

Sound familiar? It should come as no surprise to you that Bateson describes art as the human endeavor most close to nature, since art always follows the divide-and-relate rule and is persistently mindful of that middle space of relationship. It so goes, then, that when you're thinking or acting in the related way of artists, you're in the best place to comprehend the livingness in things, since your eyes are open to where it exists in the in-between space of relationship. For Bateson, that also means you can't observe nature from a distance—like artists, you have to be inside the picture, part of the story. And here's the twist: To be in the story, the story needs to be inside your head.

Bateson contrasted creatura with what he called "pleroma." Pleroma is the place where nonliving things exist. Meaning "full" in Latin, it implies a completeness to the things in it. Rocks, for example. Rocks are not dependent on living things to exist. In fact, they don't have needs at all. And it's this fact that creates a really big division between beings in creatura and things in pleroma.

A rock will change in shape, but not from its own effort or for the purpose of adapting for its own survival. The lichen on that rock, however, is constantly making adjustments in response to the unpredictable shifts and changes within its ecology and the climate around it. It's improvising, in other words. "Music represents nature.

Nature represents life. Jazz represents nature. Jazz is life," Sonny Rollins said. Bateson would wholeheartedly agree.

It's not easy to travel successfully in the uncertain world of creatura. Every step into it means a step deeper into the wilds, a place you can't predict that threatens you with no way back to a dependable holding place. To truly meet life (as Buber put it earlier), you have to be *open to life*, willing to spend your mental energy on the constant and unpredictable twists and turns of living things. You have to stay spontaneous in this terrain, the roads on every map quickly consumed by vegetation. You have to go inward—*into your self*—to travel there, too, constantly cleaning Coltrane's mirror, and thus taking your eyes a little off the world that goes on without you.

All that effort is great for feeling alive, but it's also completely inefficient at protecting you from danger. Sometimes you have to quickly make a move, and at those times your mind does a very smart thing: It shuts down too much contemplation about relationships or the livingness of the things and beings around you.

Remember that research on improvisers I discussed in the last chapter, how the part of the brain charged with self-expression comes alive when musicians improvise? That part of the brain is permitted to brighten because another part darkens. According to Charles Limb and Allen Braun, your dorsolateral prefrontal cortex dims when you play. That's the section of your brain charged with inhibiting your impulses so you can make a plan. It's the conservative part of your brain, constraining you from getting too wild; charged with *executive function*—the process aimed at *executing* things you need to get done as efficiently as possible. Much of the time, your executive function is very important. However, because its job is to inhibit you, it also will "impede the flow of novel ideas," as Limb puts it. And while you don't want to impede those ideas when you improvise or innovate in any manner, you do want to impede them when you're in an unsafe situation.

It's dangerous to muffle your executive functioning when you are at risk. That's why when we're scared, our brains run away from the playful, imaginative part of the prefrontal cortex and back to the planning and inhibiting part. Also joining in is the basal ganglia— the lizard brain, the part of us that doesn't have time for telling stories, or contemplating the interesting shapes of relationships, because it's concentrating all its energy on yelling, "Run!" In other words, when we feel scared we try to get the hell out of creatura and enter pleroma, the world of nonliving things. Or—different words, same concept—we go from an I-Thou to an I-It relationship, turning the land of living things into a land of inanimate objects.

Again, this makes sense as far as immediate survival. A mountain lion pokes it head into your tent, and your life depends on perceiving that lion as simply dangerous. Your mind of course sees the lion as alive—dangerously so—but it's bracketing out the complexity of the livingness in it, seeing the lion as one simple thing: something that threatens your life. Lion equals danger. That's the knowledge you need right then. As a result, you're planning and being efficient in your response to the lion—acting conservatively as you slowly inch your way out of the tent.

To push this point further, think of that child again, the one who plays seemingly alone, animating her toys, while minded by her caretaker. Let's say she hears a loud bang outside her house that scares her. The first thing that happens is that she stops playing and imagining with her toy, and the second is that she runs to her caretaker as a protector. No longer the source of her autonomy, the caretaker has become the very opposite: a larger, stronger being, charged with her protection, the child's job to remain frozen in her arms and dependent. What the child wants least is the uncertainty of play, and what she wants most is the certainty that she is protected, not "I'll catch you when you inevitably fall" but that she's caught, "You're safe," "Everything is fine," "I'll protect you." She's looking for an extreme kind of holding, in which her sense of security is based less on the minding of a parental gaze and more on certainty and enveloping protection. In such a situation, she might leave the toy behind, vulnerable to attack, but now a thing without life, since the child's mind has moved from imagining to efficiently seeking protection.

A concept in social psychology called *terror management theory* tells us that something similar happens to adults, and often in more massive ways than simply one brain seeing danger. Terror management theory says that the more we are afraid for our lives, the more we manage our terror by tightly grabbing cultural beliefs, narratives, systems, and symbols, and that the more we feel this terror, the stronger we hold on. Just like the child, we're looking for certainty, a sense of almost mechanic dependability and routine, and we get that certainty by seeing the cultural products of humans—things made from social ecologies—as solidly thing-like.

We fight for the status quo, in other words, rather than be creative. Terror management is based on the work of the anthropologist Ernest Becker, author of the groundbreaking book *The Denial of Death*. Becker believed that our denial of death is at the very center of our development of civilization and culture, so that a lot of what we consider great about humans comes from this denial. Yet a lot of bad does, too, especially when we're insecure. Indeed, when things get really scary for us, we place all our chips on rigid and uncurious shared beliefs and traditions or on just fitting in. The holding power of such regimes subsumes our own ability to distinguish ourselves—indeed, the whole *point* is to be undifferentiated. In the armor of conformity, we find comfort in fundamentalism (the secure certitude of unquestioned belief systems) and authoritarianism (the security of just following orders). In this rigid outer-directedness, we see anything or anyone that counters these routinized and uniform approaches as dangerous because it or they threaten to penetrate that armor.

In this state, approaching the world as something we can mold with our own originality—that is, to be playful and imaginative—becomes unfeasible, if not downright threatening. And so, for safety, we use our mental workspace to imagine the world in absolute and unconditional ways, no longer the invention of our selves, other people, or just plain nature. Since we're no longer connected to a dynamic world of living beings, we stop seeing the relational space, stop relating to this space, and disappear as distinct individuals. We also stop seeing others as the vessels for livingness. We engage with them in an alienated way, an I-It relationship, a pleroma approach in which we treat the world of the living as if it were not alive. Humans become Its and the other animals and nature become inanimate resources to exploit. And here, we're like that child in her parent's arms—but often with serious, real-life consequences—as we abandon something living, by forfeiting our play and imagination for the reassuring solidity of certainty.

You can deal with the uncertainty of livingness by imposing certainty on it, or you can deal with this uncertainty by doing the most uncertain thing: being playful and imaginative and thus improvisational and innovative. So far, Harold chooses the latter. He really meets his world. That's very true in his relationship to the tree and especially to its fruit. The apples live outside Harold, but the *perceived* livingness of these apples—their redness—lives *inside* him, as the product of his imagination. The apples and Harold are meeting in the middle space of relationship.

And here, my imagination is sparked again, the tree of life now floating in my mental workshop, bearing souls yet unseen that are waiting to be plucked by an angel and brought into creatura. Imagining the red in unripe apples, Harold is a life-giver, a conjurer of livingness. And in this he's making the hard choices, ones that resist the easier path of experiencing deadness in living things.

That all changes soon, however, as a new image enters the gates of Harold's little Eden, something cold-blooded and serpentine that curls around the apple tree.

Chapter 5

IDOLATRY

The apples would be very tasty, Harold thought, when they got red. So he put a frightening dragon under the tree to guard the apples." The dragon Harold draws is more than twice his size and "terribly frightening," its gaping mouth filled with sharp teeth. Harold stands directly in the dragon's line of vision, its eye—predator-wide—locked with his. He then backs away in fear, and his hand holding the purple crayon trembles, making wavelike marks on the page behind him.

At first, Harold doesn't notice what he's drawing with that quivering crayon, nor that he's stepping into the waves he's made. His eyes focus on the threat in front of him. As his body submerges deeper into the rough waters, he slips and suddenly realizes the new danger. But it's too late: He's "over his head in an ocean" with no land in sight. Harold's hands are soon the only things we can see of him, one holding the crayon, the other slapping at the water as he desperately tries to keep himself from drowning.

The dragon Harold intentionally drafts in front him as well as the sea he mistakenly draws behind him are both his creations, but it is as if Harold has forgotten this fact, perceiving them as separate from himself and, worse yet, turning on him and threatening annihilation. And, in this me/not-me split, the life that Harold conjures in his imagination, and feels and experiences at play, is stolen in the objects he's made, while Harold all but disappears beneath the waves.

Moon, horizon, path, field, and tree—up until now, everything Harold created was shared. Now he wants to possess the apples all for himself. They are no longer objects in his environment that he relates to but a resource for his own sustenance. Of course, we all have the right to guard our apple trees, to protect what we own, and to be able to feed ourselves. But I think with that dragon, Johnson is pointing out the dangers in placing too much value in such things, a sort of greed that is best called idolatry.

"An idol is the figure to which a person has transferred his own strength and powers," wrote Erich Fromm. "The more powerful the idol grows, the more impoverished the individual himself becomes. Instead of experiencing himself as the creating person, he is in touch with himself only by the worship of the idol. He has become estranged from his own life forces, [and] from the wealth of his own potentialities." In doing so, Fromm chillingly notes, "he transforms himself into a thing," the person's livingness transferred to the idol.

Fromm, at the forefront of what became known as the humanist movements of the 1950s, published his book *The Sane Society* the same year *Harold and the Purple Crayon* hit the shelves. His understanding of the dangers of idolization was not solely rooted in his own experience in Nazi Germany, nor in his secular scholarship, but in his earlier training as a Talmudic scholar. Unsurprisingly, when he discussed idolatry it was hard to ignore the latter teachings, especially in regard to the Golden Calf, the idol the Israelites created when Moses was on Mount Sinai, a giant statue made from individually crafted jewelry.

Idolatry comes in all shapes and sizes. You feel like you'll be more complete if you buy those jeans, and in fact you obsess a little about them, waiting impatiently for the UPS truck to finally arrive; or you take a political stand, believing it's the complete and only truth, and you have nothing but disdain for those who don't adhere to it; or you follow a religious or political leader as if they have powers beyond other humans, ignoring or minimizing their frailties; or you need that next drink, because the next one will give you that sense of well-being you seek (but will never find in this way); or you yearn for that next relationship that will finally fulfill you; or you crave the respect and admiration of others more than you rest in self-love; or you adhere to the next self-help fad, buy the newest supplement, take the next magic-bullet pill, order that face cream from the ad that popped up on your Facebook page, and on and on and on. These are all acts of idolatry. And it's as important to grasp what you're *not* doing when you worship idols as what you *are* doing. When you idolize you stop being creative with your own life. Doing so, you decrease feeling your aliveness in a state of relatedness with the world around you, because you are oriented toward the power of things outside you as life-giving.

Idolizing is a sinful act in regard to our most human impulses, since you're surrendering your sacred originality when you idolize, melting the wax of your crayons and becoming a sheeplike follower. To engage in idolatry, and thus to be alienated, is to be emptied of your species essence, to go on in life without a core. Like the Israelites, we tend to do this when we are feeling insecure. In this sense, it's the result of something close to terror management, a closing of our minds to the livingness of things, for the solid sense of something outside of us that can save us.

Fromm writes: "The frightened individual seeks for somebody or something to tie his self to; he cannot bear to be his own individual self any longer, and he tries frantically to get rid of it and to feel security again by the elimination of this burden: the self." That's what is happening to Harold as he starts to drown. Our hero is hardly a zealot, but he's being dragged down into the same uncertain waters from which zealotry is the easy escape. It would be easy for him to let go of the purple crayon right now, freeing both of his hands to stay afloat, the weight of his creative powers sinking into the depths so he can quickly swim to safety. That's what many of us fall back on when faced with precarious uncertainty.

In the next pages, however, Harold does just the opposite, forging into uncertainty by engaging the human faculty that was built to do just that.

Chapter 6

HOPING

Harold reaches out of the water and uses the crayon to draw a boat. He then climbs aboard and keeps moving forward.

In building that boat, Harold is managing the terror of uncertainty by facing it head on, deploying—not silencing—his ability to play and be imaginative to move past it. Picture him

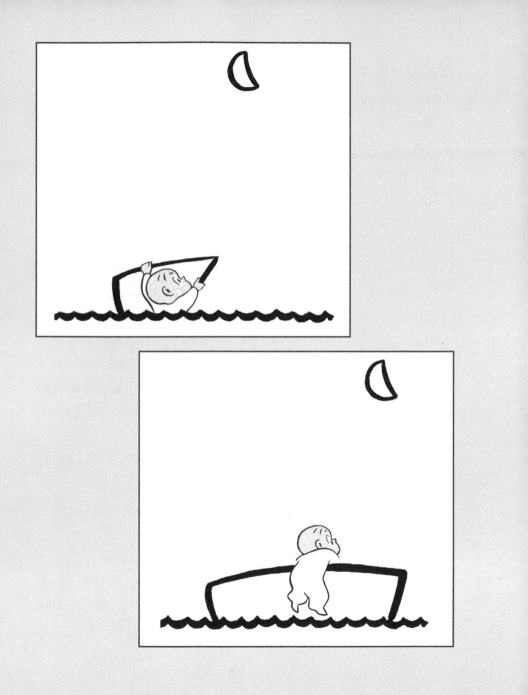

beneath the waves, devising his means to safety. Some part of him believes he can use that crayon to save himself, that his own capacity to make a life will protect his erasure. So even as Harold gasps for air, that quality of efficaciousness we find in play is still there—that sense that we are creative enough to make the world respond to our will. Under the waves, Harold in his mental workspace invents a means to reach safety.

Fighting uncertainty with more uncertainty is never easy to do. Play and imagination are not really built for getting you from A to B as efficiently as possible; a large part of their general purpose is to cause you to ponder in order to create beautiful things (among them, beautiful solutions). That means that play and imagination alone can only get you so far during crises of uncertainty, considering their uncertain, contemplative natures. You need something else to get you to the surface, something built specifically for uncertainty that pulls you to safety: hope.

"The tune without the words," as Emily Dickinson famously called it. You can't fully grasp hope through description, and it's even harder to put it into one psychological category. It's an emotion, for sure: We do feel it. But it's also a stance we take, a "state of mind," as the psychologist Susan Folkman describes it, and as a state of mind, its special function is to drive us toward a destination we yearn for, despite the fact that we don't know if we'll get there. You don't hope when you're certain, because hope isn't needed then. So while one person may be generally more hopeful than another, hope waxes and wanes depending on the circumstances. If we're lucky, hope shows up when we must cope with uncertain events. When it doesn't, we despair about the future.

Hope and despair, hope and uncertainty—you can't really talk about hope without talking about these other difficult things, and you don't feel hope without also confronting these things. That's why hopefulness is dynamic: You experience it when pushing against despair and pushing through uncertainty. It's wrong to think that only *after* you feel hope you have the confidence and energy to confront despair and uncertainty: It's the confrontation that makes for the hope, not the hope that makes for the confrontation.

Hope is difficult. Not only because it requires confrontation but because it makes things important. When you hope for something, you're appointing it as more valuable than its alternative. So when we hope, we're always risking the damage of disappointment regarding the failure to attain these (hope-made) important things.

"[H]ope serves us better than optimism," wrote the social critic Christopher Lasch. "Not that it prevents us from expecting the worst; the worst is what the hopeful are prepared for. A blind faith that things will somehow work out for the best furnishes a poor substitute for the disposition to see things through even when they don't." Hope speaks to your own agency, your own power to reach your goal, while optimism is more about waiting for a future that is promised to you.

Being original is a hopeful act, often with little optimism, because all creative activity is hopeful: Whether you're drawing a picture or drawing your life, every time you purple-crayon something, you are rendering that thing important, and you are stepping into an unknown in which you're going to need to keep going in order to get to an inevitably adapting destination.

If you were a researcher in psychology, and you wanted to assess the hope of your subjects with the most time-tested measure, you would pick Charles Snyder's hope scale. A lot of social science is like looking for black holes; you can only see a phenomenon by what's situated around it. Snyder's scale is no different. It looks at the results of hope to find it.

Synder's scale measures two things: what he calls "agency thinking," basically the sense that you can meet and succeed at a challenge ahead; and "pathways thinking," the ability to imagine a way over, under, around, through, and out of an obstacle. For Snyder, hopeful people are improvisers.

Think again of that child playing with her toys, safely minded by a caregiver. Some part of her knows that it's up to her to make things happen and feels uplifted by the fact, and as she plays, she creates a story and that story most often has moments of crises small and larger that must get solved: *The bear is going to a birthday party, but he doesn't have any clothes,* so the child makes some for him. He also doesn't have a gift, so the child gives him one of her own toys to take with him, etc.

"Even though high-hope people are goal directed, they enjoy the process of getting there as much as the actual arrival," Snyder writes. Maybe the word *enjoy* isn't the right term for this if you're hoping in a moment of significant stress and danger. But the fact remains that hope is "a creative emotional response," as the psychologists James R. Averill and Louise Sundararajan describe it. It's creative because it's the force behind novel solutions to problems.

In other words, every line you draw with your crayon is an act of hope.

The year of Harold's birth, Rosa Parks refused to move from her seat on a bus in Montgomery. Defying segregation laws, especially in Alabama, was a very serious act of hope, with little of the cheeriness of optimism. By refusing to move, she changed her relationship with the norms and laws of segregation, and by doing so painted a public portrait starkly different from the accepted one. She helped change the way buses were seen in the South in general, from modes of public transportation to sites of mobile acts of injustice.

What Parks did that day was performative and creative, bringing to life new meanings, reconceiving how others might imagine riding a bus in the South. This was an imaginative act that came from the hands of a person who along with her fellow activists must have believed that the world was moldable in some way, an act that was rooted in a belief that it's every person's right to form the life they want. Parks would never have stayed in her seat if she hadn't hoped that this dangerous act would change something, and what she did with this act was inspire hope in others. What she did was hopeful, though not happy.

The Montgomery bus boycott followed, the first large-scale demonstration against segregation and an igniting moment in the civil rights movement. Martin Luther King Jr., a young pastor at the time, was one of the leaders.

Eight years later, on the steps of the Lincoln Memorial, King gave his "I Have a Dream" speech, perhaps the greatest master class on hope in American history. The speech itself goes straight to the audience's imagination, barely a sentence without imagery and metaphor: "from the quicksands of racial injustice to the solid rock of brotherhood," "out of the mountain of despair, a stone of hope." But the speech is not just about imagining things, it's about molding and crafting experience, often out of nothing. King says:

> I am not unmindful that some of you have come here out of great trials and tribulations . . . You have been the veterans of creative suffering. Continue to work with the faith that unearned suffering is redemptive. Go back to Mississippi, go back to Alabama, go back to South Carolina, go back to Georgia,

go back to Louisiana, go back to the slums and ghettos of our northern cities, knowing that somehow this situation can and will be changed.

"Creative suffering" that is "unearned" but "redemptive," in pursuit of a change that will "somehow"—not certainly—come about: That's a very tall order. And yet this is what King was demanding of the civil rights movement: that people keep imagining where they want to go, and see themselves as effective in getting there, even if individually they're not guaranteed that they'll ever reach their destination, all of this with no absolutely clear set of instructions.

As Snyder alludes to, hope is as much about what you're doing now as it is about what you're hoping for in the future. It's a mind-set, a posture *toward* uncertainty that is spiritually or—if you wish—psychically creative, pulling at our sense of efficacy and our ability to imagine in order to pull us through.

While we don't know Harold's history or his social context in the world he roams, we can see that he conducts himself in a way that always places his humanity—his essence as a choosing, creative being—front and center, and that he holds on to his humanity at times of significant uncertainty. He keeps going on being Harold despite forces that work to the contrary. That's hope at work.

In today's nomenclature, Harold's hope-bound ability to rescue himself might be called grit or resilience, terms with little spiritual value and that capture little about our humanity. No, Harold is doing something of a much higher order than that.

When you focus on the *now* of hope, innovating ways to reach an unknown land of promise, even when every organ in your body is telling you to drop what's in your hand and just swim to the surface and tread water until rescue comes along, you're proclaiming that the more difficult way through uncertainty is worth it, because *you're* worth it. It's you that you're hoping for, and thus it's you that you're appointing as important. As you will soon read, that kind of valuing is at the root of what we mean by *dignity*.

Chapter 7

DIGNIFYING

His originality recovered, Harold draws a mast and sets sail for the next adventure. Building his own working vessel to get through uncertainty, he's teaching us an important lesson about going on being in the modern world, and why seeing originality as sacred is so vital.

You aren't mandated to appoint human originality as important and something to cherish; that's a choice you make. (If it weren't a choice, Johnson wouldn't have created *Harold and the Purple Crayon*.) But if you do make that choice, then something else immediately falls into place: Idolatry stops looking so secure. In fact, it appears as dangerous, not necessarily life-threatening but definitely threatening to the experience of *being alive*; a sort of drowning in order to stay afloat—a kind of spiritual suicide, bluntly ending your anxiety by killing your ability to remain playfully imaginative. Once you see this danger, you're going to want to hold on tightly to your purple crayon when the waves of uncertainty are cresting.

That's easier said than done, however. To stay original, even when things feel most uncertain, is to place tremendous *value* on your originality as a person, so much so that you're willing to risk feeling completely unheld. The willingness to take that risk can also be described as the drive to hold on to your humanity. The word for doing that is *dignity*.

At the root of the word *dignity* are words like *worth* and *value*. For the philosopher Immanuel Kant, things have value because humans give them value. A good term for that is *extrinsic value*—a value from the outside. When you put a price tag on something, you're assigning it an extrinsic value. Humans, on the other hand, have value as humans; they are, in this sense, *intrinsically* valuable just by being human. As a result, you can ascribe a certain value to both extrinsic and intrinsic things, or treat them as having no value, but when you place a price tag on humans, you're assaulting their dignity. The philosopher Dan Egonsson clarifies that idea, writing that simply seeing a person as fitting within the category of human being isn't really treating them with dignity; you also have to see them as alive in their humanness since "it is not a definitional truth that human beings have human status." We've seen this throughout history, and in today's headlines we see people being treated as "less than human" as the phrase goes—murdered, enslaved, abused, violated, ignored. That's why we typically use the word *dignity* to describe rights, as much as, or more than, we use it to describe a personal attribute. Whenever we treat a person or group as less than the status of human, we're violating their right to human dignity.

"Whereas recognition of the inherent dignity and of the equal and inalienable rights of all members of the human family is the foundation of freedom, justice and peace in the world"—that's the opening line of the preamble of the Universal Declaration of Human Rights, a document produced by the UN in 1948, its proclamation made urgent by the Holocaust. Eleanor Roosevelt, who is credited with its inspiration and represented the United States on the UN committee that produced the declaration, called it the "international Magna Carta for all mankind."

Many of the rights laid out in the UN declaration, mostly having to do with personal liberty, are a lot like those in the US Declaration of Independence. But the UN rights go further, the concept of dignity somewhat filling in the blank of what the US declaration calls "self-evident" truths ("that all men are created equal, that they are endowed by their Creator with certain unalienable Rights"), giving the why for the how of liberty. And once the human experience of dignity becomes the centerpiece, certain rights become impossible to ignore, the freedom from slavery and torture being the most glaring examples. There are also more subtle equity rights in the UN declaration, like equal access to public services, security, leisure, a reasonable standard of living, social protection as children, education, and the right to engage in a cultural life. All of these rights are more evident and deserving once the focus is put on dignity.

We have the right to dignity, but our dignity rests on our own comportment: how we keep hold of our originality in the face of challenges. I'd like to go back to that thought experiment in chapter one, in which I asked you to think about three things you like about yourself. Now, I ask you to add "my dignity" as a fourth (if you feel you don't have a lot of dignity, I assure you that you do have some, and I ask you to focus on that part of you). Now close your eyes for two minutes and think about these four qualities.

Welcome back after those two minutes. Did my imposition of the generic concept of dignity feel incongruent with the distinct qualities you chose, or did it make them feel more important or even more vibrant? Again, I'm hoping you think the latter. Dignity is the thing you are doing when you are cherishing and protecting your original inner core.

At the heart of this dignified effort is the ability to keep drawing from your original source: to be self-determined, able to act on one's own direction independent of the direction of others. We've been talking about how Harold could have dropped his purple crayon and swum back to shore, letting his crayon sink beneath the waves he'd inadvertently drawn. But as noted earlier, there are also many original things Harold could have drawn to make himself safe, while his crayon remained in his hand. He could have drawn an island, a raft on which to lie down and wait for the waves to push him in a direction of their choosing, or even a beach to which he could embark and wait for a passing ship to rescue him. But Harold draws a boat, then a sail for that boat so he can steer. Harold recovers from drowning in uncertainty by creating a craft on which he's the captain. If Johnson wanted to be clear about self-determination as an option, it's hard to find a more obvious symbol than a sailor catching the wind and steering in a direction he has *determined* is the best path to wherever it is he wants to go.

Chapter 8

SELF-
DETERMINING

With the sail, Harold propels himself forward, navigating his own course and thus determining his own fate. And here Harold's journey enters a slightly American current, one shared in many other cultures but that is nonetheless central to ours.

Self-determination is the framing concept of the Declaration of Independence. Thomas Jefferson forged this value into our most sacred document in its most famous line: "all men . . . are endowed by their Creator with certain unalienable Rights, that among these are Life, Liberty and the pursuit of Happiness." The "pursuit of Happiness" in Jefferson's list is particularly important—and not particularly original. He basically cut and pasted the Enlightenment philosopher John Locke's definition of happiness, which referred to the ability to make decisions that lead to the most fulfilling life possible for each individual, not the happy, zippy, cloud-nine kind of happiness that comes about when your jeans fit perfectly again or you find a twenty-dollar bill on the street. In this way, while the independence declared in our founding document is a pronouncement about our separation from England, it's also a delineation of a new set of rights for its citizens, in which the independence of each person is sacred.

Self-determination oxygenates the American spirit, circulating through the very heart of our democracy. It's a kind of commandment from which we can judge our allegiance to national ideals and, often more important, our sins. At the founding of our country, only about twenty percent of the population was granted the basic right of a self-governed nation: the right to vote. As the decades have passed, the struggles for self-determination—for African Americans; for women; for ethnic, religious, and racial minorities in general; for immigrants, the LGBTQIA+ community, and those with disabilities—are the central thread in any story about American progress. All these movements aim to allow for the unfurling of a person's original thoughts, that billowing sail powering them toward a more preferable destination. Martin Luther King Jr. refers to the promise of self-determination in the second paragraph of his "I Have a Dream" speech. "In a sense we've come to our nation's capital to cash a check," he proclaimed. "When the architects of our republic wrote the magnificent words of the Constitution and the Declaration of Independence, they were signing a promissory note to which every American was to fall heir. This note was a promise that all men—yes, Black men as well as white men—would be guaranteed the unalienable rights of life, liberty and the pursuit of happiness."

Self-determination can get a bad rap. It's often perverted in the United States, twisted into a kind of individualism that defies the vital importance of community life and interdependence. It's the gunpowder for violence in movies, from early Westerns to *John Wick*; the selling point to suburbanites for gas-guzzling SUVs; the distorted catalyst of militia groups; and the reason why your kid doesn't want to be seen with you at the mall. When people refuse to wear masks during a pandemic, putting others at risk for the sake of their right to govern their behavior, they are participating in the ugly side of self-determination.

But while self-determination has its problems, especially when one person's self-determined life impedes or limits the self-determination of another's, it is also a central triumph of the Enlightenment. If we handle it right—by not getting too rugged with our individualism—self-determination can, in fact, bring us to our deeper selves. It just takes a lot of sturdiness to do so.

"Freedom makes a huge requirement of every human being," wrote Eleanor Roosevelt. "With freedom comes responsibility. For the person who is unwilling to grow up, the person who does not want to carry his own weight, this is a frightening prospect." In order to grasp the helm of the craft we've drawn, we need confidence that we can depend on our original impulses and ideas.

Cornel West writes:

The interplay of individuality and unity is not one of uniformity and unanimity imposed from above but rather of conflict among diverse groupings that reach a dynamic consensus subject to questioning and criticism. As with a soloist in a jazz quartet, quintet or band, individuality is promoted in order to sustain and increase the creative tension with the group—a tension that yields higher levels of performance to achieve the aim of the collective project.

You can't come up with a better description of a pluralistic democracy than West's. This kind of government doesn't just promise the promotion of individuality; it fundamentally demands that the people involved bring their originality to the gig.

As mentioned earlier, *The Lonely Crowd* portrayed three particular character types, each one matching certain demands of their time: tradition-directed, inner-directed, and other-directed. For the authors, the tradition-directed kind of culture died out, or grew diminished, with the emergence of the modern world and its need for people to be more agile in the face of change, no longer living by previously set rules and traditions. This opened up a shift to a more inner-directed character. Inner-directed people are basically psychologically self-determined, depending on their own inner gyroscope— self-reliant, as the transcendentalists called it during the very era that demanded this form of character.

According to the authors, inner-directedness was a central cultural mode in the United States, eventually giving way to other-directedness, an orientation toward what other people are doing and how they're behaving: conformity, to put it all in one word.

Other-directedness is great for the working of a well-oiled machine, aimed toward material progress and consumption. You need people who will trade the expression of their originality for fitting in if you want a workforce willing to fill menial jobs aimed at the mass production of more and more uniform objects and services. You also need them to feel a sense of anxious comparison with their neighbors to get them to buy these things.

"What is the 'social character' suited to twentieth-century Capitalism?" asks Erich Fromm (noticing the same trends described by David Riesman). "It needs men who co-operate smoothly in large groups; who want to consume more and more, and whose tasks are standardized and can easily be influenced and anticipated. It needs men . . . willing to be commanded, to do what is expected, to fit into the social machine without friction."

In an other-directed culture, being inner-directed is almost revolutionary. It takes the kind of person the transcendentalists dreamed of to stay original in such a culture, a person who depends on their own inner life to guide the way. This is what they were writing about when they wrote about self-reliance, and they saw clearly the problem of other-directedness as the seductive alternative to what they valued, those "lives of quiet desperation" lived by other-directed people. "Do not go where the path may lead, go instead where there is no path and leave a trail," wrote Emerson, offering advice Harold would readily take.

A group of American social psychologists who study traits associated with personal self-determination believe that psychological self-determination is central to maintaining motivation in the face of threats and challenges, and to our overall psychological well-being. Their research gets at the fine fiber of what it means to be self-directed, and touches, too, on what the transcendentalists were talking about. Introduced by Edward Deci and Richard Ryan in the 1970s, self-determination theory (SDT) posits that people are more able to sustain their drive toward goals, and to feel more fulfilled in life, when they are intrinsically, rather than extrinsically, motivated. In other words, we find satisfaction in the pursuit of our goals, rather than in achieving goals to comply with the demands of others or for an external reward like praise. Self-determination is all about trusting our gyroscope of intuition, imagination, and impulse.

For the SDT folks, intrinsic goals fit into one of these three universal needs: autonomy, competence, or relatedness. When we are inner-directed, we are always directed *to* something, and that something is deep, in a Lockean kind of happiness. I think it's fair to say that via the boy with the crayon, we've covered the first of these three needs. Harold soon takes care of the other two.

Chapter 9

MASTERING

After a while of sailing, Harold lands on a sandy beach, draws an anchor, and disembarks. He doesn't know where he is, but the beach reminds him of picnics and that makes Harold hungry, so he sketches a picnic blanket on the beach with nine of his favorite pies, and then he eats a piece from each one.

Harold puts the mast in mastery on these pages. He is self-reliant in a material sense, for sure—a boat, a blanket, a meal. But he's also psychologically self-reliant, undefeated by his scrape with the dragon and the sea, forging ahead with little doubt about his ability to face what's to come without knowing what that will be. And this is not just a beach he frantically drew while drowning; this beach was *reached*.

The psychologist Albert Bandura famously calls this can-do

mind-set *self-efficacy*: the belief that you can complete a challenge, and that even if you *can't* complete it, you have the competence to recover from the failure. It's a stance in which people feel that they can ably take on "the courses of action required to deal with prospective situations," as Bandura describes it. In turn, Bandura also calls self-efficacy *self-belief*: To be self-efficacious is to believe in yourself because you believe you can be effective in the world.

When we play in the presence of others who are minding us and animate our toys, we're practicing our efficaciousness. Our first interactions with our caregivers are about efficacy, our gesture creating a smile in return from them, another bringing a breast or bottle to our mouth. We are doing something that gets the response we intended. Then in school, as we master the ABCs and our times tables, we're building more self-belief. As we get older, self-efficacy parallels our developing self-reliance, each step potentially inspiring us to feel increased belief in ourselves. And here is where actual, material self-reliance (the ability to navigate our world) and psychological self-reliance (a belief that we're able to do this successfully) come together. The more you become competent at things, the more you will believe in yourself in general, and the more you believe in yourself, the more you're willing to take on challenges that potentially raise your confidence.

The preeminent developmental psychologist Erik Erikson described something similar to the idea of self-efficacy in his work on the stages of life, one being the struggle between industry (actually doing things, and succeeding at doing them) and inferiority (a lack of self-belief, the feeling that you can't competently move through life). For Erikson, when we don't feel efficacious, we feel we are less-than, incompetent to get our needs met and do something valuable in the world.

I have my own story of this struggle. As a child, I had all the markings of a potential Harold, an industriously creative kid who was always inventing something. I also couldn't read or write very well, and I was horrible at math. As school demands increased in those areas, so did my sense of inferiority; soon my confidence shattered when I was labeled with a severe learning disability, marked as faulty and malfunctioning at tasks I was expected to master.

The learning-disability narrative is behind me now, but the experience of feeling inferior remained with me for decades, slowly diminishing as I built trust in myself as an adult who can pay bills and competently partner with another to provide for my family. Here's the point of my story: As a child I was in good shape as far as my self-belief, then I wasn't, and then, eventually, I was again. My experience of feeling inferior was caused by my inability to master things that were conventionally considered important for my age, along with the disability label. What brought about my recovery was gradually mastering those things I'd been told I couldn't handle. That's how central a sense of mastery is in regard to self-belief. Whatever you've been given as a young child to build the sense of your own efficaciousness only gets you so far, since your self-belief also depends on your ability to be competent as you develop. That belief isn't about just your ability to figure things out when you face a challenge, but also your ability to figure out what to do if you fail at meeting it. The latter part is just as, if not more, important.

Let's say you never fixed a bike before. You pull your old one out of the garage and set to work. You have a general sense that you'll figure it out, and that confidence not only gives you the guts to undertake the project but will grant you real momentum when it comes to making the repairs: There is little distracting noise of self-doubt as you read the instructions, and with each step you successfully follow, you build more belief in yourself.

Yet here's the interesting thing: You may not recognize it at the moment, but that initial confidence in yourself and its growth is based on a quiet belief that everything will be okay if you *can't* get the bike to work, and that you'll come up with a proficient solution. "I'm competent enough to fix this bike" and "If I don't fix this bike I'll crumble into a mess" don't go together. You can't have the first if the second is loudly lingering.

"I can do it" and "I'll still keep going even if I can't do it": Every act of originality is, by definition, something unproven with uncertain results, and the chance of failure is always present. To venture into originality takes faith in your ability to master a task of something untried, in part or—more powerfully—in full, and a belief that you'll still be standing if you fail and remain willing to try to be original again.

Most simply, you can't be creative with your life if you lack confidence. That makes self-belief a kind of self-perpetuating type of holding, both cheering you on and promising to pick up the pieces if you fail. You're doing a lot of parenting of yourself when you have self-belief, since *you* depend on *you* as a reliable source of trust and safety. In this sense, self-belief is about confidence in the truest sense of the word, moving through life with (*con*) trust (*fid*) in yourself.

"Trust thyself: every heart vibrates to that iron string," wrote Emerson regarding the importance of self-reliance. So far, Harold's story follows his growing trust in himself as he masters his world. At first, he's only got squiggles, then a few lines, then a moon to give him enough security to wander, then a path to explore on, then a tree, then a dangerous challenge he meets, then—from meeting this challenge through his own skills—a growth spurt into a self-determined life in which he steers a vessel of his making, seeking out new lands, anchors himself, and puts food on the table. And as his confidence builds, he's able to face the challenge of each new stage in his maturity. His trust in his play and imagination to guide him forward, his confidence in his ability to withstand challenges to his integrity by acting with dignity, and his conviction to stay self-determined—all of these mind-sets depend on Harold's own sense that he is dependable. He couldn't do these things if he didn't believe in himself. Nowhere is this more true than in his ability to hope.

Self-belief is at the center of hope, since it is the same thing as that agency thinking that Snyder defines as the core of a hopeful mind-set: "I can do it" and "I'll still keep going even if I can't do it." Thus, our ability to forge ahead into uncertainty requires that we believe in ourselves. Hope, in other words, requires faith, since every time we take the uncertain path we are also taking a leap of faith. That makes the ability to be a self-believer really important. Without faith in ourselves, it's very hard to have hope.

As Harold's faith in himself grows, the crayon keeps proving its trustworthiness, too, and thus its advancement as an effective instrument coincides with Harold's growth as an efficacious and hopeful person. Helping Harold get closer to his livingness, his crayon is a "convivial tool," in the words of the great social philosopher Ivan Illich.

Let's look at the dictionary again: The word *convivial* means "with" (*con*) "life" (*viv*). According to Illich, "Convivial tools are those which give each person who uses them the greatest opportunity to enrich the environment with the fruits of his or her vision." Sound like that crayon?

Not all tools are convivial, and progressively we're losing the ability to master our tools. With an increase in the need for specialized-knowledge training, the increasing reliance on experts to fix things or answer questions, and then, of course, the increasingly bewildering world of automation and technology-generated solutions, our sense of mastery over life is considerably threatened. Prophetically, Illich discussed such a doomsday:

Elite professional groups . . . have come to exert a "radical monopoly" on such basic human activities as health, agriculture, home-building, and learning, [robbing] . . . societies of their vital skills and know-how. The result of much economic development is very often not human flourishing but "modernized poverty," dependency, and an out-of-control system in which the humans become worn-down mechanical parts.

By looking at the process of commodification in regard to tools, Illich is telling us that the creep of alienation is greater than just selling us things, or even controlling how we work: It is taking hold of the very items we use to be efficacious in the world. As a result, it becomes increasingly difficult to engage in activities that bolster our self-belief. When that goes, we end up feeling like we're unable to get our needs met, like we are helpless, unprotected: Yes, unheld.

Research on the biopsychosocial (BPS) responses to challenges and threats supports this point. In this research, a challenge is defined as pursuing something we think would be good for us, that we believe we have the physical, psychological, and social resources to achieve, while a threat is defined as also the pursuit of something good, but we don't feel confident that we have these same resources. Let's say you're climbing a hill in the snow toward a cabin that is well heated by a fire. You see the walk as challenging as long as you have confidence in the resources supporting you (a good jacket, a belief in yourself, the knowledge that others are there to support you). But if you perceive yourself as lacking in these resources, you experience the cold as threatening. That means that a challenge is only a challenge and a threat is only a threat depending on how much faith you have in the resources around you. The research into BPS theory shows that two particular social psychological resources are like challenge/threat switches, deciding which way we perceive that hill: our self-efficacy and our sense of control over our lives. Or, to put it in a way that reflects on our current discussion, the less you feel you can master the world, the more you feel the world is threatening.

And by now you know about where we tend to turn when we feel threatened: away from a creative approach to life and toward something certain-seeming. We tend to bow to an idol, conform or consume, in order to feel we have protection and guidance when we perceive ourselves as unable to manage our lives on our own. We anxiously scramble for external resources, seeking something solid and dependable outside ourselves, since we don't have faith in what is inside. The more we do this, the more it limits our ability to develop self-belief, and we enter a vicious cycle, in which we increasingly depend on others in a dependent way.

"People need new tools to work with rather than new tools that 'work' for them," wrote Illich. The idea that we need tools as partners in a collaborative goal of extending our original reach into the world makes Johnson's choice of the purple crayon fantastically important and, actually, radical.

When children first encounter *Harold and the Purple Crayon*, it's the crayon that seems magical. But on a closer read, it's clear that it's no magic lamp, flying carpet, wizard's wand, miraculous ring, or enchanted slippers with powers detached from Harold, already animated before it reaches him. No, the crayon is a tool he uses convivially, his hand, wrist, and arm playfully doing the drawing, his imagination creating the design. While Harold deploys the crayon to perform the magic of creating a world, it's really Harold who is imbuing the crayon with powers.

The same can't be said the other way around: Without the purple crayon, Harold would just pick up some other tool and bring it to life—he's proven to be quite efficacious with the things around him. Harold's the epitome of handy, both made by and making by hand. With something new in his grip, he would need to patiently hone this tool until he found it trustworthy. But in the end, it would become an extension of Harold, filled in with color just like he is.

On that beach, feeding himself with the pies he's made, Harold has a lot to be proud of. I see those pies as a kind of celebration—all of his favorites. To eat the pies, Harold sits in place for the first time in the book. For a moment, a least, he's not exploring and not creating. He's at rest. Perhaps he's resting on his laurels. In many ways he deserves this.

Yet, sadly, something is askew.

Take a close look at that last image on page 119, the one with the pies in front of Harold on the blanket, each with a piece eaten. Focus your eyes for a second on the figure of Harold. He's holding his stomach, smiling and reclining. Every indication is that he's full. Now look at the entire scene, with all those partially eaten pies filling the frame, and Harold off to the side. To me, Harold looks far from satiated. In fact, he looks emptier than he's ever looked, his eyes fixed on those pies as if he's considering another serving.

Do you know the experience of being so stuffed with food that you feel empty? I do, and I see that feeling on this page. In fact, to me that smile on Harold's face seems forced, as if he's trying to convince himself to be happy. And here's why this picture of celebration seems so false to me: Harold is dining alone.

Chapter 10

LONELINESS

If you lay out a blanket on the grass in a park, and you place food on the blanket only for yourself to eat, with no plans for guests to arrive, is that a picnic? You could say it is, just like you can say, "I'm having a party for myself." But it's not quite a picnic, just like it's not quite a party, if you hold it alone. That's what makes the image of Harold and those pies so disquieting: He's trying to simulate an experience of connectedness with the most important ingredient missing. It's a portrait of loneliness.

John Cacioppo, one of the founders of the field of social neuroscience—the study of the brain as a social organ—describes loneliness as "perceived social isolation." Perception is important here. Remember our discussion earlier about social supports, and how perceived social supports—the supporting others you carry with you in your head independent of geography—are the fuel you need for facing threats and challenges? Cacioppo's understanding of loneliness is a sort of opposite version of that: the perception of being disconnected from others, independent of how distant or few or plentiful your social contacts are. It's portable emptiness in the same way that social supports fill you with portable others.

Loneliness is not easy to cure. Cacioppo argues that increased social contacts don't necessarily lower a person's perception of isolation and may even increase it (the person feels apart from an even larger group than before), and he doesn't believe therapy is completely helpful. Instead, his research argues that a certain *kind* of relating to another is the key: that you have to both bring something to the meal and be willing to digest what the other has to offer in order to feel less lonely.

Let's return to that child playing in the presence of her caretaker and think about what she's actually doing with the toys she's animating. She cares for them, coddles them, and, if they are trucks or cranes, imagines she is transporting and manipulating things a larger community might use. To put it another way, the child is living in a fantasy world in which she's valued as someone who can contribute, practicing what it means to feel connected in adulthood, which involves what Cacioppo describes as mutual aid.

This is an evolutionary thing. We come from tribes and clans, and tribes and clans have little patience for deadweight. Cacioppo describes the feeling of loneliness as similar to physical pain: It's warning you about something. What it warns you about is the danger of being left behind. That's why loneliness and stress go together—isolation having been hardwired as dangerous, the stress hormone, cortisol, floods your body—and why prolonged stress due to loneliness causes such a deteriorative effect on your life-span. It's also why the feeling of being on the outside can actually hurt physically, as the parts of the brain that respond to the smallest hint that you're being abandoned by the group are the same as those that light up when you feel physical pain.

Cacioppo claims that there is no real term for the absence of loneliness, other than *not-lonely*. I think there is: belongingness. When we contribute, we feel that we have value—we're needed, and when we are needed, we feel we are also part *of* the group. That makes Harold half right about his picnic. He's spread out the blanket, put plenty of food on it. He just needs guests to eat what he has to offer, and to offer something of themselves, too, for him to feel like he belongs.

The evolutionary purpose of perceived isolation is important to understand, but if we focus on loneliness only as the signal that we're in danger of losing the protection of our group, we can lose touch with something more spiritual. Around the time of Harold's inception, the theologian Paul Tillich wrote that "sin is separation." What he meant by this is that we stop feeling our beingness—which he associated with God, and something close to what I've been calling *livingness*—when we don't experience ourselves as related. In other words, when our picnic is set for one.

As we've discussed, all living things metabolize the world around them and return something to it. Harold's blanket is a potential site for the mutual relatedness and interconnectedness that brings us to life, but only if guests arrive, turning it into a step to the larger human ecology, instead of a place to eat—and waste—too much pie.

"Loneliness seems to be such a painful, frightening experience that people will do practically everything to avoid it," wrote the psychoanalyst Frieda Fromm-Reichmann in 1959. All around us, there are quick and potent ways to fix this sense of disconnection that don't require the complex work of actually connecting to others, drugs being the most glaring one. I'm one of those who believes that addiction and overindulgence are attempts to connect, desperate moves to experience the feeling one gets when one belongs. Endorphins, which are opioids the body naturally produces that are related to lowering pain and causing an overall sense of well-being, and dopamine, which stimulates and drives the experience of pleasure, along with the hormone oxytocin, which lowers stress, are all activated when you feel connected to others. That's why when we are disconnected we feel out of place and unwell, our bodies telling us we're in trouble, and why the stress caused by loneliness ties with high cholesterol and smoking as a cause of heart disease. Sylvia Plath described loneliness as "like a disease of the blood, dispersed throughout the body so that one cannot locate the matrix, the spot of contagion." She had no idea how scientifically correct she was.

In fact, the brain scans of people who are high on drugs and people who are feeling attached to someone else are virtually the same. But we can also find the high of connection in other problematic habits, like overeating, hypersexuality, addictive shopping, and consuming just to consume. All these things give the chemical rush of relatedness without any demand for mutuality, and most often with a much greater immediate high than a hug or a night out with friends.

Personally, I go immediately into a carb-coma after just one piece of pie. But nine? It does seem as if Harold is trying to satiate more spiritual and psychological pangs than those of hunger. And as he moves from one kind of pie to another, he's seeking to end the pain of his emptiness with just the right filling. The addiction psychiatrist Gabor Maté uses the Buddhist concept of "the hungry ghost" to describe this process of gorging ourselves—with food, with consuming, and with all kinds of pleasures—in the futile attempt to feel fulfilled. Part of that gluttony is spiritual and part of it is evolutionary, since our bodies are telling us we need to hoard as much as possible when considering the possibility of being left behind, all this in the context of a hypercommercialized world in which products are sold as a promise of satiation—a candy store of synthesized belonging.

Think about it: How many commercials on TV and on the Web surround their products with halcyon scenes of belongingness—the family who visits Grandma through Alexa, the wedding party in their Subaru, the Little League coach able to volunteer his skills because of his arthritis medications, the spouse flirting at a picnic, the husband ready with his Viagra. As I write, there's an Amazon box in the recycling can beneath my desk with the words "You're never ALONE when you have boxes to open" printed on the side. Could there ever be a statement both so enticing and so wrong?

In the modern world, we are rich in things that are packaged as delivering belongingness and poor in "social capital," as Robert Putnam puts it in his aptly titled and influential book *Bowling Alone*. Social capital is the "connections among individuals—social networks and the norms of reciprocity and trustworthiness that arise from them." It's found in places of worship, often after the sermon when people mingle, and in guilds and clubs and, yes, bowling leagues.

The loss of social capital is what leads to an epidemic in loneliness in many Western countries in particular because it removes our ability to join others in ways that are mutual. Like Harold, we depend on entering the middle space of relatedness in order to feel alive, and yet the ability to feel related—connected in eminently collective ways that are easy to access and holding in their coherence and durability—is no longer a simple thing.

Writing in *A Biography of Loneliness: The History of an Emotion*, the British historian Fay Bound Alberti argues that the chronic feeling of loneliness we're talking about is a rather new thing that didn't really exist much before the nineteenth century. In fact, the word *loneliness* rarely shows up in English literature until the 1800s. (*Robinson Crusoe*, the eighteenth-century novel that launched a thousand tales and images of being stranded on islands, never mentions loneliness.) This is because social capital was abundant in earlier times, with traditions, shared languages, edicts, and strict norms making mutual aid something that felt as natural as breathing. And if you were ostracized for an offense, you had to find some way back to mutual aid or perish.

Loneliness can be considered an injury of secularism, metastasized by capitalism. Yet being less tradition-directed also has its benefits, since traditional ways of life carried immobile systems of oppression and power, a cohesion often based on defining what is righteous through defining deviance and punishing those deemed irregular to keep the community in line. Traditional cultures are mechanical in this way, as Émile Durkheim described them, prescribing rote ways of doing things, with little room to do them differently. Belongingness is all around, but originality in such groups only goes so far, if at all, and is typically shunned or punished. Modern cultures, on the other hand, are organic, according to Durkheim, more permitting of inventiveness and change, and holding innovation and progress as important values. In the modern world we've thus struck a bargain in which we trade the abundance of accessible belongingness for a greater chance to be original. We still feel the need to belong, and to do so with originality we need the sense of holding that belongingness brings us, but we have to seek it out and put effort into getting it.

The tragic nature of loneliness is that if it is not addressed it breeds more loneliness. Cacioppo's research shows that people who experience "perceived loneliness" for long periods of time become paranoid and distrusting of others, highly sensitive to what they see as additional signs that they don't belong. In this sense, we can see the conspiratorial thoughts and paranoia of others as one result of loneliness. It's also not hard to imagine that someone who wants to solve their loneliness might seek out groups that are formed around these features, feeling they belong in a shared experience of suspicion. This is the search for union—a kind of dangerous form of oneness I describe later—not by comprehending the middle space of relationships but by eradicating it.

Putnam makes a claim about the loss of social capital that somewhat supports this point: "People divorced from community, occupation, and association are first and foremost among the supporters of extremism." Thus the sense of being adrift and disconnected leads individuals not only to gluttony and addiction but to joining anything that makes them feel like they are a part of something bigger than themselves, and often a part of something that is tradition-directed in hyperdrive: fundamentalism, authoritarianism—anything that's certain about beliefs and clear that those who don't hold them are the enemy (that righteous/deviance dyad of traditional groups). In these situations, people fill their emptiness by being outer-directed to the extreme, getting high on the fervor of the mob.

Harold on his blanket is the farthest thing from this, of course. He's just chowing down, like so many of us do when we feel lonely. But something very important, other than friends, is also missing from this picture, its absence a message about what we need to belong in the modern world and the effort required to get there.

Take one more look at the image of Harold on the picnic blanket: For the first time in the book, the purple crayon is nowhere to be found.

Chapter 11

RELATING

He hated to see so much delicious pie go to waste." So Harold finds his crayon and draws "a very hungry moose and a deserving porcupine" to finish what's left of the pies.

Harold has gained a sense of belongingness by creating something that has value to others. And here, the three drives of self-determination—autonomy, mastery, and relatedness—come together. In making his own meal and feeding himself, Harold has autonomy as a person, and he gains a sense of mastery, the confidence that he can not only make things happen but make them happen in a manner that expresses his value as a dignified person.

Now his value comes to fruition as he feeds others, creating relationships with them. He belongs because he's engaged in mutual aid, the moose and the porcupine removing the waste he would otherwise have left behind, while nourishing themselves on food expertly made by Harold. In many ways, it's a perfect image of belongingness and its relationship to our human and natural ecology. It's how a picnic should be.

But something else is going on here, something that relies on the crayon's return to the palm of Harold's hand. Harold doesn't draw a magical moose and porcupine who mindlessly serve him with their powers, nor does he see them merely as a moose or a porcupine—standard, generic representatives of species he could check off in a *Peterson Field Guide to Mammals*. Instead, he uses his purple crayon to imagine their specific inner lives—one "very hungry" and the other "deserving"—and in doing so, he enters into the space of relatedness with them.

This is a bigger deal than it may seem. While you might take it for granted, it's not at all easy to grasp what's going on in the minds of others. They are just so complex, don't even understand themselves completely, and are usually loath to fully let their guard down. The best you can do is get an approximate picture of what's happening up there. It's more art than science, this figuring others out. And yet the ability to reach across the threshold from me to not-me depends on you trying to do just that, since the key to entering a true human-to-human relationship with another depends on your capacity to comprehend their distinct perspectives, inclinations, and intentions. If you can't do that (knowing up front there will never be a hundred percent certainty), and they can't do the same for you, the whole interaction leans instead toward I-It, an experience of each other as more like things, split off and unrelated.

When Harold takes an educated guess about the inner lives of his newfound friends, he's doing something well rehearsed by children when they use their imaginative and playful faculties to animate toys as unique beings. To a child, that toy they bring to life is imbued with its own original experiences of the world—its own feelings, wants, needs. Adults use the same faculties as children to figure out what's going on in the minds of other humans. They imaginatively welcome these minds into their mental workspace and then consider them, letting them play within the workspace, to finally form a picture of what's going on. Psychoanalysts call this process *mentalization* (social psychologists call something similar *theory of mind*).

Our ability to mentalize is quite literally a crowning achievement for us humans, the part of our brain that sits at the crown, tasked with this very difficult challenge. Our neocortex is the newest invention in the animal kingdom and the ratio of its mass to the rest of our body is the greatest of all that think. It's what makes us most human, the rest of the brain leaning more toward lizards. There are many evolutionary reasons for this large amount of gray matter other than mentalizing, but mentalizing is very important to our development as a species.

Like I wrote earlier regarding the importance of play, we are the animal that regularly collaborates to invent. Sometimes the people we collaborate with are present, or we're playing off of existing cultural material created by others. There are all kinds of instincts activated when we do this, but much of our inventive collaborating isn't instinctual; it's driven by effort and choice. We aren't geese; we don't automatically fly in formation. This makes us the most disordered of all the species, never quite predictable. The odds of making the right choices, creating good things that help and beautiful things that connect us, and generally not killing each other has a lot to do with our ability to mentalize: to see the opportunity and the danger in all the other minds that surround us.

Mentalization is not a binary transfer of information: a "she frowns equals she's sad" or "he smiles equals he's happy" sort of thing. Instead, it's jazzlike, forcing you "at all times to address what other people are thinking and for you to interact with them with empathy and to deal with the process of working things out," as Wynton Marsalis describes his genre. Like jazz, mentalization isn't a Vulcan mind-meld. Far from it: It's one distinct mind trying through its own original lens to understand another distinct and original mind. And that's what makes it the key to relatedness, since it's about the relationship between two or more individuals, not a merger of them. It's about dialogue in this sense: a meeting between separate "mes" that becomes a sense of "us."

Like playing jazz (and all kinds of play), mentalization occurs at a point of optimum arousal—a moment when we aren't slacking off but are alert and engaged. And, as with these sister processes, it dies quickly if we're too aroused—stressed, in other words. When that stress blocks our ability to effectively mentalize, we become "mind-blind" (as the theory-of-mind people put it) and this often leads to perceiving the intention of others as threatening, even when they may have our best interests in mind—that switch from challenge to threat, flipped, as I described it earlier.

Johnson explores the way in which failures to mentalize cause us to feel threatened in a particularly revealing way, almost like a science experiment. In round one, Harold created his first creature with a mind: the dragon. If you go back to those pages and look closely at the dragon, you'll see that it never actually makes an aggressive move toward Harold; it's just doing its job guarding the apples, frozen there like a sentry, its eyes surveying for danger, its mouth warning anyone who may want to take the fruit from the tree beside it. The dragon is very much on Harold's side, here, keeping something nourishing and life-giving safe for him. But then Harold becomes mind-blind to the dragon's intention. Placing himself in front of its frightening gaze and gaping mouth, he misinterprets the dragon as life-threatening. Unable to nourish himself with the apples he so intensely covets, he becomes increasingly stressed and then perceives threats from all sides. With the porcupine and moose, he's going to try this task again.

Harold has done a lot of work on himself since his encounter with the dragon, building his sense of hope and dignity, and gaining a general belief in himself as a self-determined individual. He's also just finished a large meal of pies. He's more secure this round, buttressed by psychological and physical resources. He needs this security, since the creatures Johnson places in front of him are not exactly comfy ones. In fact, in real life, they are often quite threatening. Porcupine quills are sharp and strong enough that they can not only pierce your skin but drill so far into your body that they can penetrate organs, even your brain. And anyone who has ever come across a moose in the wild is immediately struck by their ominously gigantic size (some weigh more than fifteen hundred pounds). The most immediate reaction most of us have when encountering a dangerous animal is to quickly create a safe distance between us and them, to back away like Harold's retreat from the dragon. But Harold stands near the porcupine and moose. And he does so because he has enough resources to ponder their internal lives in a very complex way: more complex, actually, than what I've described so far about mentalizing.

Just perceiving that the moose and porcupine are hungry and deserving does not automatically make them unthreatening. To the contrary, most of us would consider ourselves in danger if we were sitting between a starving animal and the food it feels it has the right to eat. Thus, for Harold to see the benign nature of the creatures in front of him, he needs to do a little more work than just perceiving qualities in them. And what he has to do is what we all do when we mentalize well: imagine how they mentalize him. This is where Harold failed with the dragon, his mind blind to how it was eyeing him. And it's where he succeeds with the moose and porcupine, conducting the eloquent task of minding minds that mind him.

This very complex feature of mentalizing isn't just central to getting along with strangers but integral to feeling held. Think for a second about your experiences of holding in your own life. When you feel supported by others, even (and especially) when they aren't in the room with you, isn't that support all about the fact that they keep you in mind? "You were in my thoughts today," "I was just thinking of you," "My prayers are with you": These are the things people say when they want to comfort you, letting you know that they have welcomed you into the home that is their mind. Such words are only words, however—things Alexa or Siri could say—if they don't conjure an image in your head of you existing in theirs. Again, holding is a mutual, collaborative event, a psychological embrace in which you actively engage, not passively receive the comfort of someone else. And your part in that embrace has a lot to do with your ability to see who you are in the eyes of others.

Strange but true: The thing we need to do in order to engage with other people in a related way, and thus to engage in our humanity, doesn't come easy to us and requires that we feel secure—yes, held. And here we land on logic that is seemingly chicken-and-egg, since we need to feel secure in order to mentalize, and our ability to mentalize requires that we're held enough to hit optimum arousal but not feel too stressed.

Look at the image of Harold picnicking alone before his new companions enter the scene. He does seem lonely. Now, just like you did in chapter two, put your thumb over that moon. For me, the image without the moon evokes a real sense of dread. Sure, Harold is smiling, but he appears starkly isolated, disconnected from anything that can ground him. Take your thumb off the moon. Harold's still lonely but not quite alone: no friends, no crayon, he's still held in the glow of the moon. We know that the moon is somewhat independent of Harold already, the one object that goes on from page to page once it is initially drawn. From this, it's easy to ascertain that it's minding him in its light, looking down on him from above in a comforting way. But the moon is still also a product of Harold's imagination, regularly conjured there on the page: He's placing himself inside its glow. There's real hope in that mutual embrace since Harold now has enough security to do the mental work of welcoming strangers into his life.

We all need something solid, dependable, and preestablished like this above our heads if we want to connect with others in moments of relatedness. And, of course, if we are lucky, we can get a strong dose of that from good parenting: a solid sense of being minded that continues in our lives long after our parents are gone (the hormone oxytocin released by our mothers when we are infants actually drugging us into trust before we can mentalize). But that's also a lot of security to hang on the individuals we carry around with us. To move through life, we need some sense of security in the environments around us, not just the introjects and social supports we carry. And here again is our need for that eminently collective thing, a shared source of reliability, made durable by shared experiences of its holding in our communities large and small. We can find this in the enduring customs and traditions of our ancestors, as well as in the neighborhoods that came before us, our connections to familial lineage, religious rites and rituals, and any number of other practices and behaviors that build a sense of commonness under which we roam while feeling minded.

I'm reminded here of the Zulu greeting *Sawubona*, which translates to "I see you," as in "I see you as a person" and "I see your humanity." What a completely dignified way to say hello. And yet it's more than just something two people say when passing each other on the street. It's a tradition, connected to a past, so it is also saying "*we* see you, and by seeing you, you are a part of *us*." How profoundly important it is for all of us to feel this in our lives: "I'm witnessed in my existence" within a community of minders. Now *that's* belongingness, the true antidote to isolation. It's also a finite resource in the modern world.

Traditions in flux, our lives untethered from our ancestors, the chronic encouragement to feel we are materially deprived, the pressure to conform instead of contribute something of our own unique being: At no time in human history has the pool of social things that make it easy and possible to hold another's mind in our own been so low, while the demand for each of us to do the sophisticated work of mentalizing is so high. As I've repeatedly clarified, play and imagination give us the best chance to experience a deep and lively existence. But an understanding of how integral these two faculties are in mentalizing tells us that they are even more important than that, especially now. In a world in which the moons of traditions and customs are harder to come by, we have to depend on our mentalizing capacities if we want to cohere as a society and get along. When we can't pull it together enough to hold the mind of another in our own, we stop experiencing others as intentional, original, and imaginative creatures. We're then on the path toward dehumanization, with all its profoundly dangerous consequences.

This leaves us with stark choices, each resting on our ability to stay imaginative and playful in our connections with the world. Harold makes the right one. Bigheartedly holding the inner lives of his new friends in his head and resisting the pull to see them as simply a means to an end, he says, "I see you," and they do the same. Harold's able to enter this related space because he's become reliant on himself, which allows him actively and assertively to bask in the glow of others, knowing he's in their minds as much as they are in his. That, as you'll see later, is really the trick in going on being in the modern world. For us moderns, the onus of feeling held rests in our own sturdiness, rather than in the sturdiness of unquestioned rules and norms. We can connect with others and connect with them deeply, and we can do so in new ways that enhance our experience of ourselves as original beings. But our relatedness depends on us.

Chapter 12

RISKING

Harold leaves the moose and the porcupine to look "for a hill to climb, to see where he was." Quickly realizing that the hill isn't going to be high enough, however, he begins to illustrate a mountain slope, and then, his crayon barely in front of him, sketches the incline as he climbs toward the summit. Reaching that peak is crucial because, tired and feeling that he "ought to be getting to bed," Harold is hoping that he can locate his bedroom window from the perch of the mountaintop. He is precariously elevated when he gets to the top, his

head near the upper edge of the page, a thin-air emptiness in front of him and below. The ledge beneath Harold's knees only extends so far, leaving little space between him and a deep, paper-white chasm. Harold is now risking everything on his ability to keep drawing. One false move and he'll plummet.

What does originality get you? For starters, the potential that you will experience your own self right where you are: a distinct being, drawn original through relationship. In this in-between space, things will feel Coltrane-immediate and transcendentally awakened—your eyes wide open. And what will you see as you look out from the heights of what you have drawn? Abhorring a vacuum, and always wanting coherence, there's a very good chance that your mind will try hard to fill the undrawn expanse with concrete images of your future, your own "long straight path," paved in your mental workshop. But what happens if you somehow resist that urge for coherence—for horizons, sidewalks, and beaches—and just look ahead into the whiteness? What's there then?

Nothingness.

At arm's length, just past your crayon—beyond all the symbols you use, the references you make, the stories you tell, and the values and philosophies you believe in—is a blank page that goes on forever. This is not the in-between space but a whiteness with no bounds, no purple lines to create a distinct form between them. In fact, it is formlessness incarnate, both the unfathomable space before Harold comes into being (the *prenatal abyss,* as Vladimir Nabokov called it) and the unborn future that lies beyond Harold's grasp.

While nothing is everywhere around you, you rarely notice it, just like you rarely notice the white of a page. Why? Because nothingness is a terrifying prospect. Not only does it mean you are helpless in finding some fixed and certain meaning to life, and that your life is also unimaginably minuscule, but this big nothing raises an issue that is certainly a big something: your own death. The material end of you is the only "knowable" nothingness in an unknowable universe, so it makes sense that you mostly look away, "tranquilizing" yourself "with the trivial," as Søren Kierkegaard describes it.

"The irony of man's condition is that the deepest need is to be free of the anxiety of death and annihilation; but it is life itself which awakens it, and so we must shrink from being fully alive," wrote Ernest Becker. Our cultures, he believed, are built to avert our eyes from the awareness of uncertainty and death, and as we increasingly leave traditions and customs behind, our attempts at avoidance become more furtive, habitual, and unmanageable. "Modern man is drinking and drugging himself out of awareness, or he spends his time shopping, which is the same thing," Becker warns. You can add to this list the sins of separation described in this book, problems that arise when you take a pleroma approach to a creatura world. Idolatry, alienation, dehumanization, conformism, and authoritarianism— these are all a form of denial through certitude, and the products of fearing the blank page.

Being original relates to that fear, too, but in a different way. When you act in an original manner, you're attempting to outsmart nothingness and death by creating coherence and by being as alive as possible within all the relationships you draw, among them creations that you hope will last beyond you. Originality, in this sense, is more death-defying than death-denying, in two meanings of the word: It makes you alive in defiance, and it places you at risk of falling into the terror of nothingness.

When you grab hold of the purple crayon, you see that the only way through uncertainty is to have the courage to keep drawing, keep forming your own unique animated world. By doing that, you take the risk of acknowledging what's there (or, better put, *not* there) in front of you. There's a seeming contradiction here: Sometimes people feel their lives are meaningless because they have no future. In fact, we have a future only when we commit ourselves to creating our own world through our efforts to be original. This means admitting something to yourself, and perhaps to others: that we as individuals are the meaning-makers, and the world that exists just past our reach never was and never will be the maker of meaning. It's up to you to take hold of your true livingness, because no one else can or will.

To be original is to act in "good faith," as Jean-Paul Sartre called it, to move forward being aware of your own accountability and, in that, to always be aware of the nothingness that surrounds you. He called the opposite of this "bad faith": your attempt to see yourself as without agency, maneuvered by forces outside you. The sins against sacred originality come from this mode of being, from what I referenced earlier in regard to Sartre: a spirit of seriousness in which one views the world as in default mode, as an existence preset in the past, present, and future—a way to avoid uncertainty, in other words, with a boatload of manufactured certitude.

The opposite of this mode is playfulness. You can't play unless you see the world as malleable, and to envision the world in this way means to see that it isn't as fixed as you might assume. Once you are aware of that, you're very close to the ledge of nothingness. To stand on that ledge without the guardrails of bad faith, you have to be sturdy, willing to take risks because you believe in your competence to go on being through uncertainty, and to pick yourself up if you fall. Thus, our ability to stay playful in the face of the void has everything to do with the internal resources Harold develops as he matures; the capacity to be a held, imaginative, masterful, and dignified self. Above all, to have hope.

As I discussed in chapter six, hope is the mind-set that takes us through uncertainty with our sacred originality intact. A combination of agency thinking (*I can do it!*) and the ability to imagine on our feet, finding alternative pathways when we face unforeseen roadblocks, hope is built for encounters with blankness and uncertainty. Yet it is also brittle and easily injured.

Remember, when we hope, we assign importance to things—they become less trivial, in other words. That means there is significant risk when we hope, because hope brings us to a summit from which we can fall into despair once we notice that we lack what we deemed important on the ascent. Hope is exponential in this sense, because the more we hope, the higher we go, the higher we go, the more importance we give the things we hope for, and thus the farther the fall into a sense that we can't get the things we need. Hope is the mind-set you need to keep you on that ledge over nothingness, but it's also the thing that created the mountain where that ledge rests, and thus it brings you to a risk that can end up injuring your sense that you can master your life.

Goals unattained become messages about whether you are capable of mastering your life. Thus, when you hope, you are pushing through uncertainty while at the same time risking that you will feel less sure you can do so next time around. ("Fear cannot be without hope nor hope without fear," as Baruch Spinoza wrote.) In this sense, hope, when dashed, has the potential to injure your self-belief and to thus cause you to freeze regarding the choices you have to make to create the paths around barriers. Hope, in other words, requires faith, and yet hope is the thing that can also hurt it.

The sequence above, of Harold climbing to the summit, subtly captures all of this, illustrating the real risk of hoping high.

With Harold's new wish to get home, Johnson introduces the only backstory in the book, doing so late in its pages: that this child comes from somewhere, a house with a bedroom window. At first, this goes unmentioned in this sequence. Harold just draws a hill to survey what's around him. But when the hill is not enough, and he draws a mountain, Johnson explains why he has to get higher: "If he went high enough, he thought, he could see the window of his bedroom." As Harold stretches to draw the summit, we now know his hope: to be in his house, in his room, in his bed. In this we see that moment of hope when something is appointed as important,

more clear and vital than before Harold started climbing. And once
returning to his bedroom is rendered important by his hopeful ascent, he more clearly knows he lacks the comfort of that room. So
much so that he's willing to get right up to that edge of the cliff to
find it. He's also willing to leave the moon behind and below him,
and obstructed by the mounting hope he's drawn, this holding
source is now less accessible. Everything is precariously dependent
on Harold's mastery of his crayon, a life-giving dream either attained
or crashed by what he does next.

And then it happens: Fixated on the blank whiteness, Harold lifts
the crayon from the path and slips, and he is "falling, in thin air."

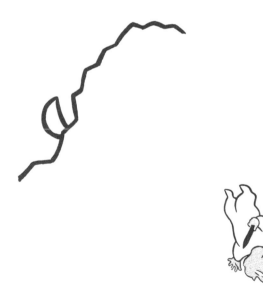

Chapter 13

RETURNING

You know what happens next . . .

When he was drowning, Harold held on to his crayon to draw a ship. This time he pulls himself out of danger by drawing a hot-air balloon to arrest his fall. Soon he's peering over the side of this contraption, leaning much like he did on the cliff as he vigilantly searches again for his bedroom window. Harold "had a fine view from the balloon but he couldn't see his window. He couldn't even see a house." To solve that problem, Harold takes his crayon, draws a house, then lands in front of it.

When did Harold decide to return home? It's really hard to say, since Johnson sort of springs the idea of a homecoming on us. In fact, we didn't even know Harold came from *anywhere* until Johnson

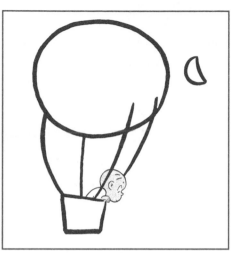

mentions Harold's home late in the book. From what we knew, it looked like Harold just appeared, abracadabra, on that preface-like title page, and then invented his world for the very first time as he moved forward on his journey. Now we know something quite different: His journey wasn't only about forwardness but about *awayness*, too—an adventure away from the confines of long straight paths. The first sequence in the book, where Harold creates a world of coherence, is still a kind of genesis, bringing something brand-new into the world, it's just a more typical beginning than we may have thought—one in which characters lived lives before the story began.

In fact, once we learn that Harold comes from somewhere, his tale of originality begins to fit into an ancient and thus thoroughly unoriginal motif. From Odysseus, Ralph Ellison's *Invisible Man*, and Jane Eyre to Tom Sawyer, *Alice's Adventures in Wonderland*, and Max in *Where the Wild Things Are* to Little Red Riding Hood, Buzz and Woody, and countless other characters in stories, Harold is on a hero's journey.

The hero's journey is most closely associated with the famous literary theorist and mythologist Joseph Campbell, who believed that there were classic stages to such narratives, spanning all cultures. In fact, Campbell described the hero's journey as the central monomyth of all cultures: one narrative structure that each culture fills with its own characters and stories. (In Western culture, think Moses and Dorothy Gale and you'll get the point.)

I'm allergic to any word with "mono" in it to describe things across cultures, but it is hard to ignore just how much the plot of *Harold and the Purple Crayon* follows the stages that Campbell describes as part of a monomyth. There's a "Call to Adventure" at the very beginning, where Harold takes off on the "long straight path," with his crayon as an aid to help him on his way; a "Road of Trials" he masters before he can return home; and much more up ahead that would spoil the story if I told you right now, all fitting neatly into the stages in the cycle Campbell described.

We now know that Johnson was engaged in a traditional practice when he wrote *Harold and the Purple Crayon*, playing freely within the sort of well-worn structure Branford Marsalis describes in chapter two. Relying on tradition in this way, Johnson is engaged in his own freestyle version of the hero's journey, adventuring from the settled and reliable structure of a plot to bring something original into the world, only to return to this structure when the time is right and Harold is ready for the next stage.

Again, think of the child playing in the presence of another. She adventures into an animated world, knowing there is a safe place to return to, and she will only adventure if she knows this. It's a state of rapprochement, as the child psychoanalyst Margaret Mahler described it, a reapproaching, a sense that in the adventure is always the return. Of course, we've reviewed how much adults also need a sense of rapprochement. To venture forth and be original, we rely on a world that goes on without us, that is familiar and reliable, ready to welcome us home.

It's easy to get lost in a homecoming celebration, forgetting that the adventure was more than half the point. I'm thinking right now of the jazz solo, and that sense of pure delight one feels right at the knuckle between its end and the return to the melody of a standard; it's celebratory in that sense—the lush, vibrating warmth of two words: welcome home.

Sure, Dorothy repeats, "There's no place like home," but most famously, she sings "Somewhere over the rainbow," and it's the yearning of this song we remember most. A homecoming is a homecoming because we left; and we were able to leave because we knew we could or would return. That, to me, is the reason why the hero's journey sticks with us, repeated in so many myths and stories: It's about the inhale of merging and the exhale of separation, that life-giving process that sustains us if we are lucky, where we never go too far into isolation or too closely into conformity, remaining as much as we can in the in-between, that place where our relationships render us distinct. In that, it's about livingness. It's about the repeated genesis of regeneration; clearing the "dust of everyday life," "cleaning the mirror," as our jazz ancestors tell us—the chance for a new, improvised day every time we wake up.

And from where do we awake? If we're lucky, it's from beneath the night tangle of sheets and blankets on our bed, in our bedroom, in our home. This is where we rest in order to hit the ground running the next day, caffeinated for experience. Like the child's experience of her parent as portably inside her consciousness, and like social support and a sense of community, home is one of our resources for feeling held. We are not kept in the mind of our homes, like we are in the minds of those who hold us, however, and that makes our sense of home different.

Home is a site of warmth and containment, and the experience of a world outside you that reflects something of your inner sacred personality. But home is also the site of thresholds, of windows and doors, of a place you return to and leave. When we are away from home, we yearn for it, and when we are in our home, we are always aware that we will go. The sound of home? A screen door slamming.

We can bring our sense of home with us, lugging our furniture, heirlooms, and family wherever we go. But home is a less portable experience of holding than are people. Conjure your social supports at a time of need, and there is a good chance you will feel more motivated. You won't necessarily miss them, however. But think of home, and the first thing you will feel is the distance between you and it; and from that you will feel the urge to either run back home or flee to the hills.

With all this in mind, here lie two serious problems in Harold's current pursuit. First, a home, whether physical or felt, should be a place of comfort precisely because it goes on without us, perpetually waiting for our return. So Harold can't invent one out of thin air, because a home is a home when it's solidly in place, enduring on its own, known by us as existing independent of what we do and don't do. Second, you are also not truly home when you are on the outside, since home happens on the inside. And so Harold's hope to find the bedroom window does not complete his journey home. In fact, it ends up exacerbating his sense of homelessness. Soon Harold will discover limits in the search for his bedroom window, and this will set his head spinning. Experiencing the lack of home that only hoping for home can generate, he'll be lost, desperate, and painfully alone.

We have reached the stage of climactic crisis in our hero's journey.

Chapter 14

HOMESICKNESS

Harold lands the balloon on the grass in front of a house, only to discover that "None of the windows was his window." So he sets out searching for "where his window ought to be," drawing window after window, hoping to find his bedroom in one of them. He makes "a big building full of windows," and then "lots of buildings full of windows," and these turn into "a whole city full of windows," all of them empty.

Harold has built a massive metropolitan facade here, a flat rendering without any potential for interiors. An outsider looking in, he peers in every window, but all his search delivers is nothingness framed, an illustration of what he lacks, confirmation that he's not home. His reaction? He becomes more anxious, more desperate, and compulsively—and yes, addictively—keeps drawing windows, painfully seeking a solution for his earlier traumatic fall into the white void.

Finally realizing again that "none of the windows was his window," Harold pauses and looks for the moon. This source of guiding light, so diligently holding Harold throughout the story, is now far off in the distance, obscured by the skyline and blocked from Harold's view by the window-filled building he just drew.

Without the full light of the moon, Harold "couldn't think where it might be." His drive to cure a deep homesickness—a longing for the *nostos* (Greek for "a homecoming") of his journey—has rendered him lost.

Home is not prefabricated. It comes from customs, traditions, sensations: food and fashion, smells and songs, shared experiences with family and a sense of lineage and history. No wonder that *heart* and *hearth* share the same root—both are about a comforting core inside a structure—and no wonder that Harold can't find a warm, life-giving center in these sheets of skyscrapers. Because of this, he is losing his own sense of a core, his originality forfeited for a near robotic replication of mass-produced superficiality.

Look at the first image on the opposite page, the portrait of the city. It's a picture of abundant emptiness, each building constructed from a frantic, ache-filled yearning. This image is also the only one in the book without a drawing of our hero or the moon or the crayon, the buildings having become a suffocating infestation of empty frames within empty frames. We almost lost Harold before, when he was drowning in the sea, but this time he's completely gone: *Harold and the Purple Crayon*, with neither Harold nor crayon.

The empty experience of chronic homesickness so acutely

portrayed in these pages is very much related to the modern experience of loneliness I describe in chapter ten, since social capital—Robert Putnam's theory of the bolstering "social networks and the norms of reciprocity and trustworthiness that arise from them"—is most easily fostered in shared traditions, customs, and beliefs: things that keep us rooted and held, in other words. Yet homesickness is also slightly different from loneliness, since it's less about closeness with people than it is about the loss of a sturdy place, a site of familiarity.

I want to give you an example of this loss in my own life, because it is so common. I grew up in a college town situated within Southern California's citrus belt, in a valley at the very edge of what's called the Inland Empire. We lived near the famous Route 66, which was called by its street name, Foothill Boulevard, by us townspeople. The next main street above Foothill was Baseline Avenue, and nearing Baseline, climbing the gentle slope of an eluvial fan, was a sea of orange groves reaching all the way to the foothills of the San Gabriel Mountains. The scent of orange blossoms there was pungent and thick. If you drove toward the mountains with your windows open, this scent changed, ombré-like, from sweet acid citrus to the herbal woodiness of sage and bay leaf as you entered chaparral. Like the foam at the tip of a wave, the groves ended at the foothills with acres of oak, wild cucumber, tumbleweed, yucca, prickly pear, and cholla. Higher up were a few homes where mostly artists lived, and a glorious

Spanish revival theater and artist colony surrounded by olive trees. Below all this, and below my family's house, was what we called "the village," a small downtown with a few shops and restaurants, a hardware store and a grocery. It was basically a one-street college town, colored by art, both craft and folk. Walking downtown, you were sure to see someone you knew. It shut down every day around five.

My parents moved to another part of town years ago, and when I go back to my hometown, I both return and don't. The orange groves are all gone, replaced with tract houses long before I entered junior high. But much more has changed in this town during the three decades I've been gone. The chaparral is decimated, replaced with McMansions, swaths of them reaching past the foothills to the mountains, surrounding and dwarfing the Spanish theater, now an odd site among all the sameness. The downtown has expanded fourfold, the main attraction a mall built inside the old citrus-packing plant. There are chain stores and restaurants on every corner. And the town is now a hub for nightlife, serving the vast sprawl of suburbs, once their own lands of orange groves, chaparral, and small downtowns stretching all the way from Los Angeles to the Mojave Desert.

Wistful references abound. All the new buildings downtown are built in California-Spanish style, or with rock facades representing the Grove Houses that once speckled the tracks of citrus trees. The town's color theme is orange, of course, and there are murals of orange groves on many of the buildings. Replicas of the luscious labels from citrus crates are sold in the stores. The town landscaping is nostalgic, all done in well-manicured chaparral. When I was young, we never thought of Foothill Boulevard as anything but an unattractive strip of road marking the line between the college town and the more suburban ascent into the foothills. Now there are exuberant notifications of its specialness everywhere, including cartoon versions of old highway signs proclaiming "Historic Route 66!" A new freeway parallels Baseline Avenue, cut beneath street level, its wall depicting the mountain ranges in brick.

So when I return, this is home and not-home at the same time, an experience of being without *kin*, right where kin should be—simultaneously a native and a visitor. The German word for uncanny, *unheimlich*, meaning "unhomely," captures this experience well.

"Little boxes on the hillside," goes the folk song by Malvina Reynolds, written the year of my birth:

> *Little boxes made of ticky tacky*
> *Little boxes on the hillside*
> *Little boxes all the same*

How do you get home, when all the little boxes are the same? Adrift in "unhomeliness," you may want to look inside the windows of all the boxes, seeking something familiar that belongs to you.

But even that strategy may not get you home, since we increasingly fill our houses with mass-produced things, bought at box stores, all looking the same. And often those items are simulated antiques, heirlooms without heirs, a candleholder burnished to look antique, a rug printed to seem worn, and where you sit, the wood on the chair came with predrilled holes in the surface to make it look "distressed."

Distressed. What a strange and remarkably telling word for this new aesthetic. It fits within an overall orientation to raise the dead not only in our home decorations but in our clothing, in how our neighborhoods are designed, in outdoor malls built to look like old-timey downtowns. It isn't that the past is present—it's that the past is made commercially presentable: new apartments built in old factories, new apartment complexes built to look like old factories, designer jeans with ripped knees, eyeglasses named after movie stars of the 1950s, and the resurgence of Manhattans, old-fashioneds, sidecars, and Moscow Mules at cocktail bars made to look like speakeasies. All this is tugging at the yearning to return, this very human instinct to get back to the hearth, all of it exploiting a sense of pervasive "unhomeliness," all the more so since the promised return is to a place that was never home in the first place. (I don't know about you, but I missed the prohibition years of speakeasies by a few decades and then some.)

Our deep yearning for *nostos* tempts us with this sort of nostalgia, one that the artist and literary critic Svetlana Boym calls "restorative," contrasting it to a nostalgia that is "reflective." Experiencing the latter, we are melancholy about the days of the past, even yearn for them, but the past remains the past, like my own recollections of my hometown. In the former, we want to restore the past, to actually put it back in place and live in it.

Restorative nostalgia promises a homecoming, and while you can most clearly witness its results in the human-made things around you, it's also pivotal in our behaviors, especially with regard to habitual ones we can't stop, the search for *nostos* in shopping, drugs, working too much, sex, porn, and all kinds of compulsions aimed at filling a dire need for the emotional fix that we've arrived and exist here, in *this* place. All these behaviors come up empty, however, because none of them are actually homely: They're synthetic, the opposite of a hearth. And so we keep looking, like Harold, in window after window, after window, after window, and creating more empty facades when we feel we've exhausted those we've fruitlessly searched through already. Our anxious yearning to replicate "homeliness" supersedes our impulse to be original, since originality is a threat to our desperate need to feel four walls around us; a venturing *out*, when we desperately want to go *in*.

Restorative nostalgia suppresses the hunger to express our inner lives in pursuit of something that feels secure in its supposed unchangeable endurance and reliability. It's another form of terror management—an orientation to conserve the past, not for the sake of remembering our ancestors and placing ourselves in history but to induce a sense of safety for safety's sake. And in this, the greatest threats to restorative nostalgia are change, diversity, complexity, fluidity.

All nostalgia is about a perceived simpler—and simplified—time. This is true in my own nostalgia about where I lived as a child and teen, a remembering in which only certain pieces are recollected (a word that means "to collect again"). The San Gabriel Valley formed a perfect bowl to capture the smog from LA. We had smog alerts where I grew up, when children were forced to stay inside and restrict physical activities on the worst days, of which there were many. At the edge of town was a barrio, a small section where mostly Mexican immigrants lived—the food workers, janitors, and maintenance staff for the colleges, and the house cleaners and gardeners for our homes—but who rarely entered the downtown other than for work. We had an unsaid real estate "color code," in which Black and Hispanic professionals were stealthily and not so stealthily restricted from buying houses. The sexual revolution was on, boundaries were broken, allowing for new forms of sexism, misogyny, and subjugation. Clearly my sepia-toned nostalgia is selective—I've taken the good and let the bad dissolve and drift to the far margins. If I include certain dislocating elements of my town into the memory, I can't get to my chosen sense of home. It's like a form of selective amnesia—the shadow half of nostalgia that's conveniently disingenuous. But it is also decidedly reflective: I'm not looking to restore this time. What would it look like if I did?

Such cherry-picking restoration wouldn't work if it only took place in my hometown in a *Truman Show*–like bubble, because knowing that I was in that bubble would mean I really wasn't back in time; I'd only be reminded of how false my situation was. So I would want this sense of *previousness* to occur everywhere, and I would want the people around me to live in that world, too, joining with me in this great restoration, reminded that we are together on this mission to renovate a simple model from a complex past, to make the present great again by making it as great as it selectively once was.

That's where the dire need for home can lead, to a wish for a simple time without complexity and mess, and a fury about anyone who blocks the course to get there. This orientation to return to the past is not very different from our other behavioral compulsions, these powerful urges to reach the hearth at whatever cost. It's also the central root of, and route to, authoritarianism.

"Authoritarianism appeals, simply, to people who cannot tolerate complexity," says Pulitzer Prize–winning historian Anne Applebaum. She says this wish for simplicity is placed in an "idealized vision of the past," nostalgically remembered as the time "when we were still whole." This makes the pleas of authoritarian leaders very attractive, especially nationalistic ones, since they promise a quick and simple return back home, found in a collective sense of *homeland*.

Harold is vulnerable to this seductive and false promise of simplicity. He wants what he really needs and deserves: a holding structure that is comforting and containing, and provides him with a sense that he belongs. And try as he might, he has attempted to create this, even in a world where doing so is not easy. Lost within the city, Harold's reliant holder, the moon, shadowed by buildings, his attempts to crayon a homecoming now failed, I see him as exhausted, his psychological resources sapped. It makes sense that he might seek an easy way to feel held, one without a lot of demands, something handed to him instead of made by his hands. And that's what happens next.

For the first time in the book, Harold draws the figure of another human being.

It's an authority figure.

Harold's greatest challenge is upon him. Will he keep drawing his own original path in search of his own original bedroom, or fall into the temptation of sameness?

Chapter 15

RESISTING

U nable to locate "where it might be," Harold "decided to ask a policeman" for directions to his home. The policeman, however, "pointed the way Harold was going anyway." And so Harold walked on, leaving the city behind.

In drawing the policeman, Harold comes close to forfeiting his autonomy. It's a little like his act of idolatry with the dragon, but this time he's not simply investing the figure with his powers, he's willingly and knowingly ceding authority to it over him, allowing his creation to author his next steps. In this, Harold is about to trade the kind of holding the moon provides, in which its reliability gives him the security to act autonomously, for the sense of severe containment, of just being told where to go.

In every hero's journey there is a moment of tests and temptations that the hero inevitably must pass in order to return home. This is Harold's.

When you think of authoritarianism, you likely picture a kind of government in which people have little freedom and are typically ruled by a single leader, or by a central source of power that preserves itself through oppressive means—the opposite of democracy. That's an accurate picture of authoritarianism in its governmental form. But authoritarian regimes come about because large groups of people want them, and what they want from these regimes is less about being led by a powerful leader and more about certain goods that such leaders offer. Authoritarian leaders amass power by huckstering a way of life, one that is simple in its uniformity.

To put it another way, authoritarianism is a reactionary way people deal with the complexities of uncertainty: It's a governmental form of terror management, filling our yearning for familiarity and reliability with the promise of a restored past of traditions, customs, and an existence that seems squeaky clean from a distance. It offers a key to a sense of home, as long as you're willing to leave your originality at the door and exist within rules and structures that demand you behave like everyone else.

People are most tempted to grab hold of authoritarianism when they feel "anomie," which is what Émile Durkheim called this modern sense of rootlessness, loneliness, and dislocation. This quick fix is a kind of holding that promises everything will remain soothingly the same, since nothing is more reliable than things that assuredly repeat and replicate.

"Intolerance of ambiguity is the mark of an authoritarian personality," wrote Theodor Adorno, who created an actual psychological scale to identify the personality of people who lean toward authoritarianism, called the F-scale (the *F* referring to fascism). This idea—that authoritarianism is linked to an avoidance and even repugnance of complexity—has held up strongly over the years. The work of the political scientists Karen Stenner and Jessica Stern perhaps best captures the relationship between complexity and authoritarianism. "Authoritarians," they write, "have an inherent preference for oneness and sameness; they favor obedience and conformity and value strong leaders and social homogeneity over freedom and diversity."

In linking authoritarianism with a thirst for homogeneity, Stenner and Stern are offering an explanation for why it's a diversion to see those people we associate with authoritarianism as merely unified in their tendency to hate, because it's not hate per se that drives the wish for authoritarianism. Instead, as we discussed earlier, the longing for uniformity coincides with an idealized conception of a simpler life.

Authoritarianism is the wish for coherence in overdrive. As we discussed in chapter one, you can only see something as distinct when it is in relationship to something separate from itself. This means that the more you seek to define a *we,* the more you need a *them* to point to, and the greater you want others to be your defining opposite, the more you want to divest them of the thing that makes them similar to you: their humanity. Thus, the dehumanization of others is both the by-product and the sustainer of authoritarianism, but like the authoritarian leader, dehumanization is not the psychological need that drives people to it. What they want is pure and unquestioned coherence, whereas human beings who look and act and believe differently disrupt the order they cherish. In this sense, authoritarianism flattens the middle space between the me of Harold with his crayon and the not-me of the world he draws, in order to create a sense of only us—no individual, only a clan—while at the same time widening the space between us and them.

As it turns out, a stunning percentage of people are predisposed toward authoritarianism, about a third of the populace in countries where it has been researched. This makes sense, since our DNA still carries tribal ingredients, ones that make us want to "defend and aggress," when things seem complex or different, as the social psychologist Stevan Hobfoll describes it. According to Stenner and Stern, "this bias [toward tribalism] is greatly magnified" for authoritarians. And, they point out, modern democracy is always in conversation with authoritarianism, since the former—with its constant promise of change—consistently threatens the psychological needs of that third who lean toward the latter. But authoritarianism isn't just a holding that only promises sameness. It purports to protect its adherents from the existential threats of play, plurality, and flexibility. The authoritarian mind is as pro uniformity as it is anti originality, and so its greatest nemesis is free-floating originality.

In 1937, the Nazis held an art exhibition in Munich that they titled *Degenerate Art*. Six hundred and fifty works, each accompanied with a description of its danger and depravity, were put on display. The concept of *Entartung* (meaning "degeneracy") dated from the late nineteenth century but had become more prevalent with the rise of authoritarianism. According to the theory, modern art (painting, film, music, sculpture, etc.) was seen as the sign of a contaminating psychopathology with potentially devastating effects on the gene pool of society. Such art was attacked for its lack of coherence, its spontaneous nature, the way it expressed the original inner life of the artist.

Jazz, of course, was seen as degenerate, which makes sense, since authoritarianism offers a decidedly anti-jazz kind of holding.

"Jazz music is the perfect metaphor for democracy," writes Wynton Marsalis. "We improvise, which is our individual rights and freedoms; We swing, which means we are responsible to nurture the common good, with everyone in fine balance; And we play the blues, which means no matter how bad things get, we remain optimistic while still mindful of problems." Improvisation and swing, rights and freedoms, a common good formed from polyphony, mindfulness of problems—these are the sweaty night terrors of the authoritarian. And thus every time we break toward a lively and original approach to the world, we are also breaking from something else: the anti-creative forces that want to hold us back from doing just that.

Lost, alone, and confused—and so very modern in his dislocation—Harold is tempted by the comfort of the kind of standardized life authoritarianism promises. And yet he's sturdy and dignified enough to realize that the police officer was pointing "the way Harold was going anyway," an indication that Harold knows the officer is his own creation and, by knowing this, is a sign that Harold is resisting the alienation of his own powers after a very short lapse into doing just that. Once Harold achieves this, he moves on, ready to face the blank page again.

Harold recovers his originality in this way throughout the book, and with increasing courage, as he resists the seductive holding of sameness, confident that he can figure out his own route. Harold chooses the more difficult road because he knows what he'll give up

if he doesn't. At any moment in the story, he could have just drawn a house and stopped there—but he didn't. His trials have given him the wisdom and strength to live sturdily in the face of uncertainty because he's learned that play and imagination bring him to life and give him coherence. He's learned that in the face of the blank page hope is the most dignified driver of fortitude, that dignity, manifested in self-determination and bolstered by the confidence mastery generates, is a sacred right. Finally, all these things lead toward his ability to feel held in the right way—not so tightly that he loses himself and stays put but enough that he feels secure to venture out (the evolutionary raison d'être of holding). Harold's ability to be held in this way began when—in the mindful illumination of the moon—he played and imagined enough to create the coherence to go on being. Now he's at another place of growth, since he's close to the completion of a circle, where all the small achievements become one continuous story, ending in a triumph.

"A foolish consistency is the hobgoblin of little minds," wrote Ralph Waldo Emerson in perhaps his most quoted statement. Little Harold's mind is far from little. To the contrary: It's expansive, open, alive, spontaneous. Look at him in the last image of the sequence above. Resisting the temptation to place his powers in someone else, he's staring up at the moon again, just like he did before when he was lost in the city. But this time it's unobstructed from his view—illuminating a simple line at his feet, as he holds a mundane tool made magical in his hand, all of this drawn within unframed whiteness. Moon, child, a crayon, and the line: He is back to his origin—originally, original.

To be original is not to walk directly to some ordered predestination; it's to saunter—a word that means both "without land" and "a trek to the holy land"—to wander curiously, with some goal in mind that will nonetheless modify each improvised step toward it. And to do that is to deal with blankness in the most courageous way, by choosing an uncertain route through uncertainty. Harold knows that every "long straight path" only gets him so far in his quest for livingness.

Emerson rightly asked, "why should we grope among the dry

bones of the past, or put the living generation into masquerade out of its faded wardrobe? The sun shines today also."

Indeed, it does.

As does the moon. And in the light of that illuminating orb, Harold now takes a step and finally saunters home.

Chapter 16

FRAMING

Harold stops drawing for a moment. Like an artist studying his work, he holds the crayon up and contemplates the moon. "Then, suddenly, Harold remembered. He remembered where his bedroom window was, when there was a moon. It was always right around the moon." He then draws a window frame, with the moon in its center. And now, for the first time in the book, he's inside.

Harold is home.

When my son was young, he would play alone (in our mindful presence, of course) in our front yard. We lived in an active neighborhood, a regular procession of neighbors, cars, bikes, dogs, and strollers passing by. As Max played in the dirt and grass with his toys, all this activity went unnoticed by him. It was as if the world outside our yard was invisible. In the evenings, however, that all changed, the invisible now acutely seen by him.

Before bed, Max loved to look out his window and watch the street below. He could "see" it now, with a curiosity about all the comings and goings because of the window itself, which framed what otherwise was indiscernible as uncontained. Max could envision the world beyond his yard better, by limiting his view of everything else.

But another thing was happening here, too, as he looked through the frame—something in many ways more important than the bracketing of vision. Max could *engage* with this world—could meet it and relate to it—because it was on the other side of the window.

When Harold draws his window around the moon, he is doing the same thing, constructing a barrier to make a threshold. And unlike the futile drawings of windows earlier, he's distinctly on the inside, where home happens. This is Harold's final lesson on coherence and especially what it means to be an original self.

Harold's window divides and defines the me of Harold in his room from the not-me of the world that goes on without him. And only by dividing Harold from the moon outside, can he have a complete relationship with that moon. Harold isn't really drawing a room in this sequence (there isn't one: just a window) but a sturdy self, someone who is solid enough to contain uncertainty and yet transparent enough to let the light of an outer world in. It's this kind of self that can feel at home in the world, even when there are less homey resources around it.

No one but Harold built this sturdy frame, just like no one drew the path that got him here and all the things he encountered along the way—the boat, the pies, the beach, the dragon and moose and porcupine, the mountain, the balloon, even those first windows and the empty city. He created all these things because he was courageous enough and effective enough to be able to keep drawing despite the fact that many of the drawings created their own dangers, ones that would be avoided if he followed the seductive calls of uniformity and bad-faith efforts to place his powers into something outside him. And each step along the way brought him to this roomy selfhood, as he built enough hope, enough trust in himself, and enough dignity to not only experience the holding of others but to be able to hold himself—to be his own, self-reliant source of fortitude.

Nowhere in time have we needed this kind of sturdiness more, as the thresholds between our inner lives and an outer world are weakened by that one-two punch of the loss of a stable sense of the outerness provided by traditions and deities, and the ravenous invasion of our interior experiences that bring commercialism and new technologies ever so deeply into what was once privately inaccessible space.

Shall I say it again? I will: There is such a thin line between the opportunities for making our life art and the dangers of dislocation and a flattening of our existence in this era. In order to take advantage of the former and protect yourself from the latter, you need to be inner-directed as much as possible, able to construct your own original frames in a frameless world, to have the "ontological security," as the social theorist Anthony Giddens describes it, that enables you to be capable of creating meaning in a space where meaning is no longer given.

If you want your life to be rich and deep and related, you need all this. But let's be clear: A sturdy self is not a necessity for your physical survival. To live a long life, you don't *have* to draw. The manufactured world around you will efficiently get you to the end just fine, without you putting crayon to paper or even lifting much of a finger. While tradition-directedness may be dwindling, the opportunities to steer clear of your own autonomy are everywhere in outer-directedness, the warm-blanket comfort of conformity achieved with the swipe of a credit card.

Living does not take a purple crayon. Livingness does, however. And the ability to bring yourself to life—an original human being living in an animated world—is the central opportunity of this age. It's offered with great inequality, but it's nonetheless there if you are in the position to think beyond your own survival: the triumph of a world in which the building of frames requires your engagement.

Karl Marx famously wrote: "All that is solid melts into air, all that is holy is profaned, and man is at last compelled to face with sober senses his real conditions of life, and his relations with his kind." Like many Enlightenment thinkers, Marx was filled with a fervent belief in the progress of a more scientific and rational world, convinced that we would reach our species essence once stripped of tradition, myth, and ritual. He was overly optimistic.

A world devoid of a hard-and-fast relationship to tradition is indeed a land of potential creativity and self-creativity, a sought-for territory in which each of us is able to meet our potential as original beings. And yet, in this, we are like the dog who finally caught the car it's been chasing, confused by what we grip between our teeth.

Luckily, we have some help in figuring this out. And that's because "all that is holy" really isn't totally "profaned," and thankfully so. When Harold draws that frame around the moon, I see him as placing it in a kind of shrine, the star of the story for one page, a beacon for a secular kind of sacredness based on the earthiest of premises: that our holiness exists in the original ways we meet each other and the world around us.

Durkheim believed that religion not only created a social bond but facilitated a "collective conscience." For him, religious practices were pivotal sites where the devout look to find shared values. We have, in this country, a "civil religion," as Robert Bellah called it, one rooted in our founding documents, which can reflect and facilitate our values in the same way. At the very center of this particularly American religion is the collective belief that there is something sacred in each of our personalities.

The architects of our constitution are rightly called framers. And while we might bind ourselves in reverence for this founding document each time we bring out the flag or watch fireworks on the Fourth of July, there are other, more resistant, less formulaic, and very often rambunctious ways we do so, too. These practices are not mediated by national symbols or blatantly patriotic traditions, and they definitely don't require formally declared pledges of allegiance.

Instead, they reach directly to our deepest values, beyond an unquestioning love of the homeland, and straight to a reverence for our original souls.

Perhaps it is no coincidence that when you mix blue and red, you get purple.

I see Harold walking beneath that moon as a kind of saint in this denomination of our civil religion. He's imperfect, he's broken at times, but he is also heroic, courageously maintaining his dignity by doing everything he can to keep himself and the world around him animated. And as he looks at the moon, now enshrined by his window, I imagine other saints looking through their windows at it, too, seeing a different version of what he sees but also a similar one in its sanctification of "the sacredness of human personality." Together these individuals form a band of Harolds that is thankfully, originally my own, the group of apostles that are part of my distinctiveness, because they are part of where I'm from in time, geography, and culture. So here are my saints: Henry David Thoreau and Ralph Waldo Emerson and Martin Luther King Jr. are looking up at that moon, as are John Coltrane, Billie Holiday, and Bill Monroe. Woody Guthrie, Joan Baez, Hank Williams, Aretha Franklin are there, too. So are Abbie Hoffman and Dick Gregory, the Marx Brothers, Mel Brooks, Bugs Bunny, and the Cat in the Hat; the Dadaists, David Byrne, and Laurie Anderson. I hear Funkadelic playing, and I see Bootsy Collins taking the lead. Joining this ragtag procession of saints are authors like Mark Twain, Dashiell Hammett, Maxine Hong Kingston, Philip Roth, James Baldwin, Lillian Hellman, Junot Díaz, and Maurice Sendak. Lowriders are there, too, with their glorious, sumptuous, and often comic style. So are all the gender benders and gender experimentalists. Paul Tillich, Reinhold Niebuhr, and Ram Das gently, tenderly join in, everyone rambling past barbecues, hootenannies, hoedowns, and mosh pits, the hot springs of Esalen, Radical Fairy gatherings, happenings, raves, block and house parties, and the AIDS Memorial Quilt with its intricately sewn panels sanctifying thousands of intricately original lives. The procession meanders past fantastically nimble break-dancing teenagers spinning on stages of flattened cardboard boxes, stops to drink from ceramic challises made by Beatrice Wood, to sit in Stickley chairs, at Noguchi tables, while listening to Ginsberg's *Howl*. Leaving behind spray-paint can footprints and the snake marks of skateboard wheels, my saints go marching for Black Lives Matter and join millions filling streets and parks, wearing knitted pink protest hats.

You certainly have your own saints. I know you do, since you live above that giant aquifer of sacred originality that knows no soil it can't spring from or seep through. You should revere these saints, just as much as it's important to revere our founding documents. Each is on a journey to make life as alive as possible, each yearns for connection to a greater whole, and each knows that the key to both can only be cut by them. It's good to meander in the moonlight with these saints, yours and mine, and to know that the moon—this eminently collective whole made of a universe of original parts—is there for you, providing enough light for your journey. If you do join, you might want to look just about knee level. There you will catch a glimpse of our hero, a gentle grin on his face, a sly reminder that he was never isolated in his aloneness but always walking within an invisible crowd, under the same moon as them, humbly doing his part.

When you do something that sets you apart, you are part of something: That's the big lesson here. You are not alone when you bring the uniqueness of you into the open. To the contrary, you not only enter the world of relatedness but you are aided by shared values with strong ancestral roots, ways of being that are as American as . . . well . . . not exactly apple pie but some confection from an exceptional recipe and served only for today. I urge you to pick up your crayon and sanctify your life with it. Not only will the expression of your originality get you closer to yourself but it will also join you to a remarkable group of moonlight travelers. And in this, you may end up sainted, a Harold for someone else.

Go ahead, break free from your isolation and join them. You might be worried that somehow you'll lose yourself in the fervor of their cause. But I promise you, they are the furthest thing from a mob.

Chapter 17

ENDING

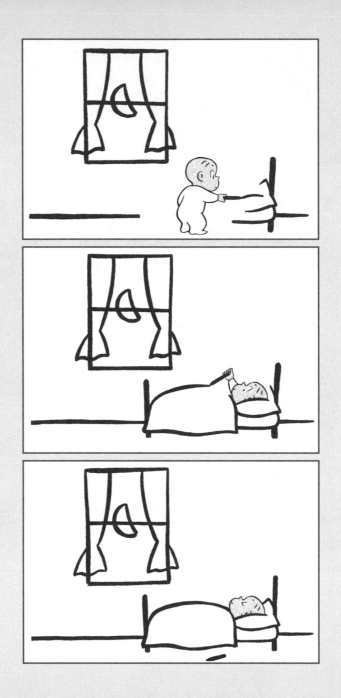

And then Harold made his bed. He got in it and he drew up the covers." Then he does the most unoriginal of things: He falls asleep. The purple crayon drops from his hand and to the floor, still within reach. Held in his home, Harold is safe enough to surrender this trusty instrument.

But only for now.

We know that when Harold awakens from his rest, he'll pick up that crayon from the floor. He'll need it as he adventures out again, leaving his home to enter another blank page.

Johnson ends his book here. I will do the same with mine, since there is little more to picture without his prose and images lighting the road ahead. Of course, my book was always an attempt to humbly collaborate with the author of *Harold and the Purple Crayon*, to enter the middle space of relationship with him by playing in my own original way with the material he created. Perhaps less obviously, it was also an attempt to collaborate with you, reader—a bashful reach across the boundary between me and not-me that cured a little of my isolation. I do hope you felt less isolated reading it, too, and that I was right to imagine you close beside me as together we walked down a path with Johnson and Harold, encountering a dragon, sailing on a boat, eating pie until we were stuffed, building friendships, searching for home, and sauntering along until it was time to go to bed.

We are at a fork in that path now, you and me, our playmates having left in their own directions just a few hundred words ago to generously collaborate with millions of other readers. And as we look out into the paper whiteness, I hope I was persuasive enough, and tender enough, to nudge you into trusting your gut a little more, to having more faith in your creative impulses, and to taking the dignified route of mastery and inner-directedness. Will you see more clearly the blessed livingness in you?

Maybe it's unrealistic of me to expect so much out of it, to think so boldly about my ability to influence you, or to presume that you need to be influenced at all. But, then again, we're talking hope here, and hope is always bold, a mind-set that steps ahead of what's realistic, there to help us think beyond the standard and play our own tune, never knowing whether the music we make will be valuable to others.

As I hope to be effective—to have left a mark, purple or not— I'm clearly hoping for myself as much as for you. And as we stand at the crossroads, the wiser of us gone from the scene, I wonder if either one or both of us will succumb to the forces of uniformity, the seduction of it and its outright coercion in our society. They are powerful, those forces, not only coming from outside us but from inside us, too, the result of our psychological unsteadiness. To be *realistic*, there's a good chance that we will succumb—at least momentarily—since conforming is the most normal thing to do.

Then again, what is normal but a conniving trick in the sales pitch for uniformity? It promises you safety and comfort when it's actually a really dangerous thing to do. Just think about the consequences of a uniformed life—the squandering of the sacred gift of your one-of-a-kind soul; isolated subsistence emptied of meaning and connection; a vacuum of a playless, artless existence; your mental workspace stuffed with the newest brands, leaving little room for original impulse; the stupefying callousness of blindly following leaders. Considering all these dangers, plummeting into the white vastness of possibility doesn't seem so bad, does it?

"My future starts when I wake up every morning," wrote Miles Davis. "Every day I find something creative to do with my life." The first part of that quote is true for all of us, and we can't do anything about that truth, even if we do everything possible to ignore the terror of the blank page. The second part, on the other hand, is up to us, that fork in the path beneath our feet, that we're standing on right now.

Where will we go, you and I?

We'll never know until we take the first step, and then the next, and the next, and the next, and the next, and . . .

I'll take that first step if you do, positioning myself right at the beginning of my path, as you do the same with yours. Look at us. We're already facing away from each other, excited and apprehensive about what's next.

Ready?

About the Author

ROSS ELLENHORN was trained as a sociologist, psychotherapist, and social worker. His previous two books focus on empowering models of psychological recovery, ones that often work in contrast to the medical model of psychiatric or pychological interventions. His career outside of writing has specifically focused on destigmatizing care for individuals who have been labeled as suffering form psychiatric diagnoses. In this same vein, Ross is a pioneer and leader in the development and promotion of community integration services, types of care that serve and empower individuals experiencing extreme events of mind and mood, while they remain in their own communities and outside institutional settings. He is the founder and owner of Ellenhorn, the most robust community integration program in the US, with offices in Boston, New York City, and Lost Angeles, and the co-owner of Cardea, a psychedelic assisted wellness program located in New York City and Treasure Beach, Jamaica.

Ross is the first person to receive a joint PhD from Brandeis

University's prestigious Florence Heller School for Social Welfare Policy and Management and the Department of Sociology.

He lives with his wife in Charleston, South Carolina, and their doors are solidly open for the wistful visits of their children, their grandchild, and anyone else who might come along.